Young Adults

Engage the Bible

push it!

Young Adults
Engage
the Bible

push it!

volume 3

United Church Press, Cleveland, Ohio 44115
www.ucpress.com
© 2002 by United Church Press

Grateful acknowledgment for permission to reprint from the following: Denise Levertov, "The Task." Copyright © 1984 Denise Levertov. Reprinted by permission of New Directions Publishing Corp. ■ Howard Gardner, *Frames of Mind: The Theory of Multiple Intelligences*. Copyright © 1983 Howard Gardner. ■ Juan Ramon Jimenez, "Oceans." Copyright © 1980 Robert Bly. ■ Lauryn Hill, "Ex-Factor." Copyright © 1998 Sony/ATV Tunes LLC, Obverse Creation Music, Colgems-EMI Music, Inc., and Careers-BMG Music Publishing. All rights reserved on behalf of Sony/ATV Tunes LLC and Obverse Creation Music administered by Sony/ATV Music Publishing, 8 Music Square West, Nashville, Tenn. 37203. All rights reserved. ■ Barbara Kingsolver, *The Poisonwood Bible*. Copyright © 1998 Barbara Kingsolver. ■ Carter Heyward, "Blessing." Copyright © 1995 Carter Heyward. Used by permission of SPCK. ■ Danna Nolan Fewell and David M. Gunn, *Gender, Power, and Promise: The Subject of the Bible's First Story*. Copyright © 1993 Danna Nolan Fewell and David M. Gunn. Used by permission of Abingdon Press. ■ Tony Kushner, "Angels in America: A Gay Fantasia on National Themes. Part Two: Perestroika." Copyright © 1992 1994 Tony Kushner. ■ Zack De La Rocha, "Maria." Copyright © 1999 Sony/ATV Songs LLC and Retribution Music. All rights administered by Sony/ATV Music Publishing, 8 Music Square West, Nashville, Tenn. 37203. All rights reserved. ■ Robert Frost, "The Road Not Taken." Copyright 1969 Henry Holt & Co. ■ Indigo Girls, "Hammer and a Nail," Copyright © 1990 EMI Music.

We have made every effort to trace copyrights on the material included in this book. If any copyrighted material has nevertheless been included without permission and due acknowledgment, proper credit will be inserted in future printings after receipt of notice.

Push It! has been designed to be used with the *New Revised Standard Version* of the Bible. All scripture quotations are from the *New Revised Standard Version* of the Bible, copyright © 1989 Division of Christian Education of the National Council of Christ in the U.S.A., and are used by permission. Occasional adaptations have been made for clarity and inclusiveness.

All rights reserved. Published 2002

Printed in the United States of America on acid-free paper

07   06   05   04   03   02   5   4   3   2   1

ISBN 0-8298-1465-5

CONTENTS

Introduction: What's the Push All About? 1
How to Use *Push It!* 5
Ideas for Deepening the Connection to the Bible 12

1. Entertaining the Unexpected 25
   Genesis 18:1-15 (Abraham and the Angels)
2. Freedom for One and for All 35
   Exodus 14:1-31 (Deliverance from Egypt)
3. Battle of the Sexes 45
   Judges 4:4-10, 14-22 (Deborah and Barak)
4. Living the Hard Questions 55
   Job 1:1, 2:1-10 (Job: A Blameless Man)
5. "I Will Be with You" 64
   Isaiah 43:1-13 (I Have Called You by Name)
6. Shaped by God 71
   Jeremiah 18:1-11 (Go Down to the Potter's House)
7. Walk the Talk 79
   Micah 6:1-8 (What Does God Require?)
8. Taste of Mercy 88
   Matthew 5:1-11 (The Beatitudes)
9. Blowing the Lid off "Fair" 97
   Matthew 20:1-16 (The Laborers in the Vineyard)
10. Who Gets What? 106
    Matthew 22:15-22 (The Question about Taxes)
11. Bearers of Justice 114
    Luke 1:26-56 (Elizabeth and Mary)
12. Called to the Table 123
    Luke 5:27-32 (Jesus Eats with Sinners and Tax Collectors)
13. Who Is My Neighbor? 129
    Luke 10:25-37 (The Parable of the Good Samaritan)
14. Faith Works 137
    James 2:14-26 (Faith without Works Is Dead)

INTRODUCTION: WHAT'S THE PUSH ALL ABOUT?

Welcome to this third volume of *Push It!* As with the first two volumes of this Bible study for young adults, you are again invited to approach the Bible with your distinctive expectations. You are encouraged to start where you are, to "push" the scripture, and then to get "pushed" in new and challenging ways.

What expectations do you bring to the Bible? Are any of the following attitudes similar to yours?

- When I read the Bible, I'll know what to do and how to live my life. It gives guidelines for living.
- It's a bizarre book, full of all kinds of visions of the world. Some of the pictures it paints of the world—the way the world should be and how people act—are important to imagine. I want those ideas floating around in my mind and gut as I figure out what to do with my life.
- I really want to know God; it's a spiritual thing. I figure the Bible is about God. It'll help me get to God.
- The Bible has always been important to the church, to lots of people in the United States and Canada. Because it seems so important, I ought to consider looking at it now. I guess I'll check it out to see if it has some real value.
- I don't know a thing about the Bible, but I am curious. I want to look at it and see if it has anything of significance to offer.
- The ways people have used the Bible seems to have messed up a lot of things. I want to wrestle with it myself and see if it says all the things that people think it says.

Push It! recognizes these varieties of experiences and expectations that you and other young adults bring to the Bible. As it leads you into the study of the Bible, perhaps you will be surprised at the attitudes and expectations that surface for you.

Push It! makes some assumptions about the expectations of young adults, assumptions you can test. At least three assumptions led to the concept of "push it" and all the pushing that goes on in this volume.

The first assumption is the concept of "push." Push is the energy that many young adults bring to a task before them—grounded in their own experience of the world. To push is to test something's truth and its relevancy for life.

Push is similar to what Tom Beaudoin has characterized as "the irreverent spiritual quest of Generation X."[1] Both society and the church teach about religious meaning through media, technology, sciences, and tradition. Young adults, as creators and receivers of that culture, often work outside the traditional box asking questions or making connections that other adults may overlook. Cynicism, irreverence, and attitude may characterize this push.

In this study guide, we understand such irreverence as a spiritual gift. That gift is evident in the expectations about the Bible suggested above—the demand for truth and relevancy. It is a gift, touched by God's sometimes discomforting spirit, that authentically demands a connection between the world today, the world of young adults, and the ancient tradition of the Christian faith. The push is also a prophetic gift that young adults may bring to both church and culture—exposing hypocrisy, demanding truth, and leading to acts of justice and love. Each session will invite you to push the text, explore your questions, and connect with your life.

A second assumption is that the Bible is a great source of religious imagination for young adults. Along with irreverence, imagination and idealism are often pointed to as vital characteristics of young adults. When you try to figure out what you want to do with your life, or with whom you want to be, or what is important to you, what do you do? You imagine. You paint a picture of your world as you see it, start to identify your calling and future, and go to work on it. Daniel Levinson has characterized the task of young adulthood as the formation of a "dream."[2] Such idealism may inspire and lead you—maybe powerfully reemerging throughout your life.

The images, stories, characters, and words of the Bible provide a stage on which to gain—sometimes by opposing, sometimes by accepting—God's biblical imagination. You may challenge the Bible out of your vision. The Bible, however, may paint an alternative imagination for you—pushing you. Perhaps you will see a vision of the world different from the injustice and violence in the world around you. *Push It!* is designed to help you imaginatively experience the Bible—to explore it with head and heart. It also is designed for you to play with, challenge, and act on the images that emerge out of study.[3]

The third assumption is the role of and need for engagement with others. Who inspires you? To whom do you look to help you figure things out? Who pushes you in a way that brings out the best in you? Whom do you want to be around to test your ideas, party, feel at home, or reveal your heart? Whom do you want to care for? As with many young adults, you may experience a shift in how you relate to others from your years as a teenager. Now others are as important to direct and shape your lifework in the world, as they are for love and acceptance. You may look to a mentor, teacher, work supervisor, coworker, or relative to push and be pushed by. At the same time, you may be a Big Brother or Sister, volunteer, or mentor to someone else expressing and testing your vision of the world. With peers at school, work, church, and elsewhere, you may both care for and push one another. You may take stands that sometimes are in solidarity with others, but sometimes stand against others, expressing the gifts of both irreverence and idealism.

When you approach the Bible, your personal interest may be foremost in your mind. You may also look at it with others—challenging others, listening to others, praying with others, and critically viewing how others live it in the world. This volume encourages you to work together with other young adults and to learn from one another. Together you push the Bible and listen to it. *Push It!* also pushes you to move out from study alone and into the world of others—taking stands and serving others.

Push It! is also part of a larger Bible study program for all ages. As a young adult component in BIBLE QUEST: A BIBLE STORY CURRICULUM FOR ALL AGES, almost all of the fourteen Bible stories and passages included are also explored in materials available for all ages.* As part of your engagement with others, consider studying the passages with persons of other ages. Try leading a group of young children or junior high youth. Explore the passages with older adults. You may discover their challenges and insights, their own pushes, will challenge and inspire you.

Whatever expectations you bring to the Bible, whatever passions you bring to life, these are spiritual gifts that may be used for engaging the Bible. The hope is that *Push It!* will help you in an irreverent, imaginative, and communal discovery of God through the Bible.

O God, you gave me life. I am going to push you to push me to make the most of it. Amen.

Sidney D. Fowler
Minister for Worship, Liturgy, and Spiritual Formation
Local Church Ministries: A Covenanted Ministry of
The United Church of Christ, Cleveland, Ohio

*For information about BIBLE QUEST materials for other ages, contact your denominational publisher or United Church Press at 800.537.3394 or ucpress@ucc.org.

1. Tom Beaudoin, *Virtual Faith: The Irreverent Spiritual Quest of Generation X* (San Francisco: Jossey-Bass Publishers, 1998).
2. Daniel Levinson et al., *The Seasons of a Man's Life* (New York: Ballantine Books, 1979), 91–97.
3. For more on young adults, imagination, faith, and the Bible, see Beaudoin, *Virtual Faith*, 155; Sharon Parks, *The Critical Years: The Young Adult Search for a Faith to Live By* (San Francisco: Harper & Row, 1986), 108–58; and Walter Brueggemann, *Texts under Negotiation: The Bible and Postmodern Imagination* (Minneapolis: Fortress Press, 1993).

HOW TO USE *PUSH IT!*

WHY USE THIS GUIDE?

Push It! is a thought-provoking guide designed to act as a springboard for your spiritual reflection. The sessions in this resource contain contemporary poems and stories, musings on current films, books, art, and music. This guide also contains some of the most dynamic stories of the Bible. You are given opportunities to ask critical questions of these ancient texts, while being challenged by the issues and concerns raised by these stories.

Individual persons can use *Push It!* as the basis for personal study or meditation. Groups will also find the guide useful as a resource for a variety of educational programs, particularly for those designed for young adults. The book may also be used as part of the program BIBLE QUEST: A BIBLE STORY CURRICULUM FOR ALL AGES.

Push It! was developed with the assumption that you bring your experiences, doubts, challenges, conversations, and hopes with you when you study the Bible. These concerns enrich that study, making the Bible relevant while pushing you to reassess some of your assumptions. Your questions about the world around you, as well as your critical questions about biblical stories, are a vital part of your spirituality. It is our hope that you will bring these questions to your study of the Bible while being open to having the Bible "push" you in new directions.

The writers of *Push It!* believe that the Bible tells the story of real people who struggled with some of the same personal and social challenges we face today. Concerns about relationships, war, social change, famine, money, inequality, and rural and urban life were as familiar to our biblical ancestors as they are to us. Discovering these connections between past and present, we may experience hope and fresh energy to address these challenges.

Each session in *Push It!* opens with an artifact of modern life—a poem, story, reflection, cry for justice, or emotional dilemma—that sheds light on the spiritual dimension of our lives. These expressions of human conflict, joy, and desire are set beside biblical stories that express similar emotions and challenges. Through questions and activities, you are invited to experience the dialogue between the past and present, between our struggles and those of our biblical ancestors. Feel free to contribute your questions and insights to the dialogue. Contrast your writing, art, and music with the biblical stories, and allow those stories to return the favor—enriching the creativity within you.

THE MOVEMENT OF THE SESSIONS

Each session of this guide begins with a title that indicates the focus of the session. The title is followed by a verse that seems to express at least one theme of the biblical story that will be explored. A modern comment follows the verse, connecting our lives with the lives of our biblical ancestors.

LIFE'S A PUSH

This section of the session starts with a story, poem, meditation, image, movie scene, song, or scenario that may connect with some of your experiences. This is followed by a series of questions that enable you to reflect on your life and the hopes, disappointments, and dreams you are facing. If you are using the questions for group discussion, feel free to omit or add questions. A short prayer is included to root your exploration in the holy and to recall that God is with you in your spiritual quest.

THE STORY

A Bible story is provided within the body of each session. Most often these stories are reprinted from the *New Revised Standard Version*, a 1989 translation by the Division of Christian Education of the National Council of the Churches of Christ in the United States.

Read the biblical story carefully, then choose a way to experience the story from the many provided in "Ideas for Deepening the Connection to the Bible" on pages 12–24. You may want to think about the ways the focus issue is raised in "Life's a Push" as you choose your method of experiencing the story.

YOU PUSH THE STORY

In "You Push the Story," you are invited to explore pushes. Pushes are the challenges you may want to raise about the Bible passages. They include questions about things that seem unbelievable, wrong, confusing, or compelling in a story. These are the questions with which you may long to confront the writers of these stories or the community they were written for.

Many push possibilities are provided in this guide. We encourage you to add your own to this list. Use them as a jumping-off point for your reflections or group discussion. Keep in mind that some of your concerns may also be explored in "The Story behind the Story" section in each session.

This guide is intended to be a user-friendly tool. Don't be afraid to make notes in the margins of the Bible story. Highlight phrases or questions that are significant to you.

THE STORY PUSHES YOU

In this section, the Bible pushes back with questions that will challenge your assumptions and provide new insights and perspectives. You will be encouraged to think about the ways the Bible offers comfort or challenge, judgment or healing. Opportunities will be provided to reexamine your beliefs and actions through the lens of the characters, stories, and faith experiences expressed in the Bible.

Once again you will be offered a series of push possibilities. However, these will focus on the ways in which the Bible pushes you. Add your pushes to this list. Take time to write in a journal about the impact of these pushes on your spiritual journey.

THE STORY BEHIND THE STORY

Each biblical story was developed in a particular context, time, and place. In "The Story behind the Story" you will learn more about the background to the biblical story. Information is provided about the times in which the Bible story was written, the community of the story's original hearers, and about the issues and concerns the story was written to address. Historical information, the meaning of words and phrases, and the ways in which early faith communities lived and functioned are examined.

PUSH OUT

Faith and biblical insight doesn't begin and end with individual reflection. It is always set in the community in which we live—both local and global. In this part of the session, you are invited to express, through concrete actions, the insights you have gained. Possibilities for social action, retreats, and community service are provided. Art, film, music, and literary suggestions are included. However, these are only starting places. Add your ideas and those of others to these suggestions. If you are participating in a group study, you may find that these push-out ideas will help you expand your study beyond fourteen weeks.

If you are using this guide for individual reflection, we encourage you to think of others in your community with whom you might share some of the insights you have gained. The stories in *Push It!* are great to share over coffee with a friend, or with someone you know who is struggling with the same issues raised in this guide.

GROUP IDEAS

There is a final page in each session that outlines ways to structure group sessions. Under "Life's a Push," you will find warm-up activities, suggestions for creating a pleasant atmosphere, and ideas for worship or centering. Group ideas for "You Push the Story" and "The Story Pushes You" include suggestions for engaging the group in push possibilities. Concrete ideas on how to lay out "The Story behind the Story" are provided under group ideas. Ways to end sessions are suggested at the close of the "Push Out" section.

INDIVIDUAL USE

There are many ways to use this guide for individual reflection. Individual persons may want to meditate on the biblical stories and the musings on modern life. Persons can respond to the push possibilities in their journals. The poems and prayers, and discussions of music and art, can also act as a springboard to one's creativity. Individual persons may want to paint, draw, or write about the ideas raised in the sessions. They may also find information and ideas that will help them with community projects that they are involved in. Those who choose to use *Push It!* for individual study should feel free to skip around the sessions, using the sections that seem to speak to them about their specific concerns.

Whether you use this guide for individual or group study, find people to dialogue with about the concerns raised here. The insights you gain are valuable and are meant to be shared in community.

USING THE RESOURCE IN A GROUP CONTEXT

There are fourteen sessions in this book. They can be used in a variety of group settings, including Bible or study groups, church school for young adults, retreats, work camps, fellowship groups, service or outreach committees. *Push It!* is also a great resource for university or campus ministry. The ideas and stories in each session can be pulled out and used either as a reflection to open a meeting or as a starting place for an in-depth discussion of a challenging topic. *Push It!* is a flexible guide that can be adapted to different settings and to various time frames.

Groups may want to share the facilitation of each session, or designate a single facilitator. Sessions can be held weekly, biweekly, or monthly, depending on the time and commitment of the group members. Your group may also wish to focus on only a few of the sessions. They may want to address particular concerns raised by these sessions (such as grief, loss, or justice concerns). The writers of this resource recommend that you feel free to use the resource in whatever way best suits the needs and concerns of your group.

Many groups take a study-action-reflection approach. This is similar to the approach taken in this guide. Opportunities for biblical exploration are provided, along with ideas for community action. Prayer, reflections on scripture, and meditation ideas are also included. These in turn lead back to more study of scripture, and the call to act in response to the biblical witness. All of this is set in the context of community—both the biblical community of ancient times and the modern community of those struggling to live out their faith as disciples of Christ.

Those who are already working in social justice or community service groups often find that they are emotionally drained by the often daunting work that they are doing. In *Push It!* a hopeful vision of social concerns and biblical values is explored. This will be refreshing to those who commit themselves to this kind of witness. It may also offer some sense of spiritual grounding for the work they are doing.

Retreats can also be designed using the sessions provided in this guide. Retreats provide an opportunity for groups to spend more time discussing the push possibilities and developing concrete responses to the "Push Out" ideas. Several sessions are ideal for retreats. The session on Genesis 18:1–15 would work well as a time of welcome to new members in a group or community. Try combining the sessions on Matthew 20:1–16 and Matthew 22:15–22 for a retreat about how faith informs our decisions about money, possessions, and consumerism, as well as how we might address global economic issues from a faith-based perspective. Another combination—Micah 6:1–8, Luke 10:25–37, and James 2:14–26—could be the basis for a powerful retreat about social justice. For a retreat on personal vocation, consider Jeremiah 18:1–11 combined with Luke 1:26–56. Also, use Judges 4:4–10, 14–22 as a way to focus on relationships between men and women. Other combinations or single sessions might jump out at you as good explorations for retreat settings, depending on the needs and interests of your group.

Expanding This Resource beyond Fourteen Weeks

Groups may wish to use this resource for more than fourteen sessions. Sessions can be broken down into two or three shorter sessions. Or if groups want longer sessions, they can add to the sessions before they break them apart. For instance, more push possibilities can be added to sessions. Multiple options for reading and/or experiencing the story can be used.

When groups are excited about the issues raised in a particular session, you may want to add a session to continue the conversation. Speakers can be invited and/or the group can create its own session outline based on the outline provided the week before.

More sessions can be developed to focus on developing and implementing "Push Out" ideas. These sessions will require planning and group input, especially those that involve learning about community service opportunities or planning retreats. It may be that your group will develop a pattern of meeting once to experience the material in the session, once to plan push-outs, and a third time to engage in the "Push Out" activity.

When your group ends its study, mark the occasion in some way that is significant for the participants. You may want to plan and share a special worship time or celebrate with a party or shared meal. Express the sense of community you have experienced together as you have pushed your spiritual growth.

IDEAS FOR DEEPENING THE CONNECTION TO THE BIBLE

You will be asked in each session of *Push It!* to read and experience the focus Bible story for that session. First, read the story found in "The Story" section of the session. Then, experience the story through one or more of the methods described below.

These methods are meant to provide variety in deepening your connection with the Bible stories. They can be used by either individual readers or groups. The thoughts, feelings, and conversations sparked by the "Life's a Push" movement of the session can help you decide which method of engaging each particular story might be most meaningful or illuminating. Experiment with a variety of methods as you move through the sessions. Also, consider trying multiple methods with the same story to extend the use of the sessions in this guide.

WHY READING THE STORIES ISN'T ENOUGH

If we bring what's important to us—our struggles and dreams, our feelings and ideas—and seek to enter its many worlds, the Bible comes alive. The Bible stories in *Push It!* challenge us to come to them with our whole selves and all of our senses. We are invited to truly relate to the characters, listen in on the questions and arguments they raise, and float the Bible's rivers of plots. That's what these experiential methods are: invitations to merge ourselves, our gifts, our personalities, and current questions into the power of the story.

The well-known professor and theologian Martin Buber once wrote, "A story must be told in such a way that it constitutes help in itself. My grandfather was lame. Once they asked him to tell a story about his teacher. And he related how his teacher used to hop and dance while he prayed. My grandfather rose as he spoke, and he was so swept away by his story that he began to hop and dance to show how the master had done it. From that hour he was cured of his lameness. That's how to tell a story."[1]

That's how to tell a Biblical story. To bring our whole mind, body, and spirit into the Bible story and then forget ourselves in its allure so that we might be transformed.

Eugene Peterson, translator of the popular, contemporary translation of the New Testament, *The Message*, writes, "Good storytelling involves us in what has been sitting right in front of us for years but that we hadn't noticed or hadn't thought was important or hadn't thought had anything to do with us. And then we do notice—the story wakes us up to what is there and has always been there. . . . The Scriptures, simply by virtue of their narrative form draw us into a reality in which we find ourselves in touch with the very stuff of our humanity, what we sense in our bones counts."[2]

Perceptions from stories bear seeds in our thinking through reading and discussion. For these perceptions to grow and take root in our lives, there is a tending, a germination that occurs through actions which prepare us to hear and see and reflect. Often transformation occurs in the midst of actions that plant perceptions in spaces where they find nurture. It's much more than simply setting our minds to the story. It is setting our whole way of being to the story.

Often the stories of the Bible invite us to take particular actions. This form of the message of God-with-us suggests the function of our engaging the message: active, creative, embodied, communal, meditative activity. Bible stories are stories of an active God woven together with stories of human activity. Consider Denise Levertov's poem, "The Task."

> As if God were an old man
> always upstairs, sitting about
> in sleeveless undershirt, asleep,
> arms folded, stomach rumbling,
> his breath from open mouth
> strident, presaging death . . .

No, God's in the wilderness next door
—that huge tundra room, no walls and a sky roof—
busy at the loom. Among the berry bushes,
rain or shine, that loud clacking and whirring,
irregular but continuous;
God is absorbed in work, and hears the spacious hum of bees, not the din,
and hears far-off
our screams. Perhaps
listens for prayers in that wild solitude.
And hurries on with the weaving:
till it's done, the great garment woven,
our voices, clear under the familiar
blocked-out clamor of the task,
can't stop their
terrible beseeching. God
imagines it sifting through, at last, to music
in the astounded quietness, the loom idle,
the weaver at rest.[3]

CHOOSING A METHOD

The method you choose for a story is influenced by a number of factors: the form of the Bible story, the realities that have bubbled up in "Life's a Push," the diversity of ways that we as humans come to know and engage the world, and the comfort level of the group experiencing the sessions.

If the Bible passage is a narrative with characters and plot, methods of acting out the story, such as readers' theater or guided meditation can be helpful. If the passage is a visionary story like the words of the prophet in Isaiah 43:1–13, you may choose methods that stretch the imagination, such as art or poetry. Some stories function inside the context of bigger stories and may require methods that allow for those bigger stories to be known. The stories of Job or Deborah and Barak, for example, will send you curiously searching the books within which they are found. A number of the stories in this volume of *Push It!* are filled with the drama of a debate, building an argument or pleading a case. The conflicts Jesus experienced with religious authorities (Matthew 22:15–22 and Luke 10:25–37) or the argument about faith without works in the book of James may be stories that lend themselves to debate or working closely with words.

Thoughts and feelings raised in "Life's a Push" can direct choice as well. Difficult, more personal themes require sensitive levels of engagement that allow participants greater degrees of safety in what they share. Joyful, expansive imagery in scenarios may suggest movement and creativity. Methods which begin with individual work will be more appropriate to themes that invite introspection while themes focused on community-building may lend themselves more to group exercises.

There will be some methods with which you will feel more at home. In a group, each person will experience different comfort levels with different methods. It helps to vary the methods. Those methods with which we are initially least comfortable can, with patience and encouragement, be those that lead us to the greatest discoveries of the story and of ourselves. Building a sense of trust in oneself, in the group, and in the group facilitator will reap rewards, as you begin to risk trying more adventuresome ways of experiencing the stories.

Differences in individual comfort levels with particular methods of experiencing Bible stories may be due to the fact that we each encounter the world with a unique mix of intelligences. Howard Gardner, in a book *Frames of the Mind*, identifies at least eight different intelligences by which persons learn and interact with the world. These are:

Logical-Mathematical Intelligence is the ability to learn through abstract symbols, the testing of hypotheses, and the search for patterns among ideas or objects. Working logical puzzles, outlining, and sequencing engage this intelligence.

Naturalistic Intelligence is the ability to observe nature, define it, and care for it. Growing things, observing nature, and working with animals are examples of this.

Bodily Kinesthetic Intelligence is the ability to use tactile senses and the body to understand things. Miming, dancing, and playing active games are examples.

Visual-Spatial Intelligence is the ability to see and create images such as drawings, maps, and sculptures.

Verbal-Linguistic Intelligence is the ability to use words in writing, speaking, reading, and listening. Storytelling, debating, and working crossword puzzles engage this intelligence.

Musical Intelligence is the ability to use sound, rhythm, and tone through listening to songs, tapping, and playing musical instruments.

Interpersonal Intelligence is the ability to form relationships with others. Playing group games, leading discussions, and participating in cooperative projects engage this intelligence.

Intrapersonal Intelligence focuses on the interior of our lives. Things like journaling, silent reflection, guided meditation, or daydreaming express this gift.[4]

Underlying Gardner's description of the phenomenon of multiple intelligences is that people learn in many ways, and no one way of learning is better than any other. We have primary intelligences that we feel comfortable using and we can also push ourselves to engage some of the others.

As we select methods for experiencing Bible stories, therefore, it is important to be attentive to the primary intelligences engaged by the methods and to strive to create a good balance of those intelligences as we move through the sessions. The goal is to allow everyone to have an opportunity to engage those intelligences that come most naturally, as well as those that are most challenging.

Ideas for Deepening the Connection to the Bible 17

LIST OF METHODS

Here are some suggested methods from which to choose:

1. USE ART.

Talk about the dominant image or images in the story and then invite artistic expression of the image or images using tempera paint and brushes, linoleum block printing, crayons or markers. For example, after reading a passage such as the Deliverance from Egypt in Exodus 14:1–31, discuss images like the pillar of cloud, the pillar of fire, the separated waters, and the people of Israel walking through the sea. Suggest that participants focus on one or two of the images for their artwork.

For a quick activity with paint, have participants focus for five to ten minutes on the feelings that a story evokes and then paint with attention to color and texture rather than detail.

Use clay to express feelings or images that emerge from reading the story. Try shutting your eyes as you work, letting your hands do the creating and only glancing at what you are doing periodically. Clay can also be used to create characters in the story, capturing the identity-shaping action or gesture of that character. Or, what would a contemporary expression of Caesar's coin mentioned in the story of Jesus and the religious authorities in Matthew 22:15–22 look like in clay?

With just about any medium, you can depict one of the scenes of a story or create a personal reaction to the story. If you are the facilitator, be clear about the focus of the art assignment so people feel comfortable starting out. Allow fifteen to twenty minutes for the work. You may want to put on quiet music. Emphasize that being artistic is not the intent of the activity, but simply being as authentic as possible. Allow time to share results as a group when people have finished. Invite the group to offer an opportunity for members to explain their creations without comment from others.

2. Examine the Story's Structure.

Make sure each participant has a copy of *Push It!* Have colored pencils or highlighter pens ready. In a group, people can work in pairs or as individuals.

First, underline words that are either the same or similar with the same color to see if there is any pattern to their use and placement in the story. Look also for phrases that are the same or similar and underline or highlight them. Sometimes passages are structured with repetition around central themes of the story.

If it is poetry, is there any set meter to each phrase? Read the passage aloud to see where the short and long syllables land in each line. What words or syllables are emphasized?

If it is a story, what are the different scenes? Where does the tension develop and where is the tension resolved if it is resolved? Who is the protagonist in the story?

Circle words that you want to know more about. Using a concordance available from a library's biblical studies section—a resource book that lists all the words used in the Bible and where they can be found—look up the other instances in which your circled words appear. Pay special attention to multiple occurrences in the same book of the Bible or similar books. What does the use of these words in other passages suggest about their meaning and importance? You may also look up the words in a Bible dictionary.

Finally, if the story comes from Matthew, Mark, or Luke, see if it can be found in one or both of the other gospels. If so, it's known as a "gospel parallel." These stories are collected and shown side-by-side in *Gospel Parallels*, edited by Burton Throckmorton (Nashville, Tenn.: Thomas Nelson, 1952). Compare versions of the same story in different gospels. Sometimes a story is longer or shorter than it is in another gospel, with details changed. What is added or left out or presented differently? These distinctions may be hints to the special point the gospel writer may be making.

3. Read the Passage in a Variety of Ways.

Try reading the story by going around a circle with each person reading a verse. Or direct several voices to read the story through in its entirety, leaving a time of silence between each reading. Or designate different voices for the characters and one voice as narrator in the form of readers' theater. Or suggest that the men read one verse and then the women read the next verse and so on, or one side of the room and then the other side like a choral reading. Try reading the story with different kinds of music in the background or in different settings, such as outside, in a room with an echo, in a confined space, or in the dark with participants sitting around a candle. Try shouting out the passage and then reading it in a whisper. Direct one voice to read and then the rest of the group to repeat each phrase, mimicking the inflection of the solo reader. If you know someone who is familiar with American Sign Language, invite her or him to sign the passage while someone else reads it aloud. Try reading the story by replacing the pronoun "he" for "she" and the word "father" for "mother" when referring to God. Discuss what is revealed by the different ways of reading.

Here's an idea. The verse from the Micah passage in session 7, "Do justice, love kindness, and walk humbly with your God," could be used as a mantra offered in different voices and different settings.

Also, don't forget about using different methods of reading if you want to explore more of the context of the story from the book of Judges or Job's story in sessions 3 and 4, respectively.

4. Act Out the Story.

Acting out the story could take the form of mime, role play, or skits. Through mime, participants can personally experience each of the characters in the story. Spread the group out across a large open space for this activity, but have participants stay close enough so that everyone can hear the facilitator. As the facilitator introduces each of the characters, participants mime that character's actions as she or he imagines them. The story of the Good Samaritan in Luke 10:25–37 works well for this. After the story is read, the facilitator names the man fallen victim, the priest, the Levite, and the Samaritan for the group to mime. Give participants a chance to talk about how they felt in each role. What was it like to mime the characters? Why did they choose the gestures they used?

Role-play is like mime but people take on the speaking parts of characters as well as their actions. Sometimes role-play helps capture the moods of particular portions of stories. Perhaps you could attempt to capture the mood of Mary's visit to Elizabeth in the story from Luke 1:26–56.

Or spend some time exploring Sarah's mood as she laughs behind the tent flap in Genesis 18:1–15. Try different textures of laughter to express any number of feelings that might explain such an outburst in the context of this story.

The cycle of stories in this volume of *Push It!* suggests debate or courtroom drama as an experiential method at various points. Job seeks to put God on trial. He receives testimony from his friends, and a powerful rebuttal from God to his own arguments! The carefully crafted rhetorical styles of the Matthew 22:15–22 and Luke 5:27–32 stories of Jesus' encounter with the religious authorities work well as debates. Consider staging these with different voices taking on different sides of the argument. What gestures and inflections fit each point? Where would the opposing parties position themselves?

Be sure to discuss these experiences. Have people share how playing the various roles made them feel; what insights the experience brought them; and what new appreciation of the stories they may have gained from it.

Creating skits is especially effective if you are spending more time with a passage, such as in a retreat setting, where groups can take time to prepare. Different groups could prepare the same story with a different treatment. One group could prepare a pantomime, another a drama, another a musical, yet another a comedy. Groups could change the setting of the story. For instance, the parable of the laborers in the vineyard (Matthew 20:1–16) could be adapted to various contemporary workplace situations.

Emphasize that the purpose of the activity is not to create an award-winning production, but to explore the motivations, feelings, and actions of the characters—and to elicit responses to the story from the group.

If participants are not ready for these kinds of activities, invite them to sit with their eyes closed and imagine being each of the characters as excerpts are read from a story. Invite people to keep their eyes closed as they respond to discovery questions like, "In a word or phrase, how do you feel as Job?" Or, encourage participants to make entries in a journal or notebook after an imagining experience.

5. Work with Words.

Photocopy the story and cut it up into words or phrases. See if you or the group can rebuild the story by piecing the words and phrases back together in the right order. If you can do that, then try playing with the story a bit. Move phrases around—what happens to the meaning of the story? You can also pull out key words and write them on a piece of paper or newsprint, one word per piece of paper. Together, brainstorm related words, images, phrases, or synonyms for the key words, recording them on the same sheet of paper. What fresh insights into the story emerge as you explore the words more fully?

As a different way to work with words, look for a pattern to the argument that James creates in the story from his letter found in the last session. How might you diagram the logic of the argument?

6. Write Your Own Words.

Paraphrase the story in everyday, contemporary language. If you're part of a group, have everyone share their paraphrases. Or write a parable, poem, prayer, or litany based on the story. Make it an individual project, a project done with partners, or a group project. Writing works especially well following an experience with one of the other methods of engaging the story because people have more to draw upon.

Certainly the sayings of Jesus in Matthew 5:1–11 could have new meaning through careful paraphrase. The song of Mary in Luke 1 is a beautiful basis for poems, songs, or litanies to be created for worship. The parables of Jesus can also be rewritten with contemporary references.

7. Pair with a Painting or Poem.

Choose a painting, photograph, lithograph, poem, or hymn that shares a dominant image with the story and talk about how each amplifies the meaning of the other. What feelings are expressed through both or in one but not the other?

Find a painting that suggests the story of Abraham's hospitality to the visitors in Genesis 18:1–15. Look for photographs of someone who could very well be Job. Explore some of the volumes of images of Mary and bring several to the story of her birth announcement and response.

8. Pray or Meditate.

Read the story slowly either silently or aloud. Do you notice any word or phrase in particular? Meditate on that word or phrase. Allow it to touch your life. What feelings, thoughts, memories, or images arise in you when you sit with it? Read the story again, reflecting on the invitation to action this word or phrase extends to you. Commit the phrase to memory.[5]

In the quiet space of prayer, let your imagination vividly carry you to the places and scenes of the story. When you return to the group, discuss your discoveries and feelings.

9. MOVE.

The story from Micah says to "walk humbly with God." If you are physically able to walk or move, spend several minutes walking or moving around while repeating this "mantra" to yourself. If you are participating in a group, have someone read this passage from Micah found in session 7 repeatedly as the group members move around in private meditation.

Experiment with the kind of prayerful movements of hands and body that would express the words of Mary in Luke 1:46–55.

Consider what kind of motions the potter makes when visited by the prophet Jeremiah in Jeremiah 18:1–11. How would the potter rework the vessel?

Groups should be mindful of different levels of mobility when engaging stories through movement.

10. DIALOGUE WITH A CHARACTER.

Choose a character in the story with whom you would love to have a conversation. Record your "conversation" on paper. Ask the character to tell you about herself or himself. Attempt not to control the character's voice, but let it speak freely as you imagine the character. Try to relate to the character, whether or not you identify with him or her. For instance, imagine talking to Job. What would you ask him? How might he respond? What's interesting is that, in writing down this "conversation," you are creating a dialogue with an inner aspect of yourself named Job. What questions and "aha's" does that bring into your faith journey?

---

1. Quoted in Parker Palmer, *The Active Life* (San Francisco: Jossey-Bass Publishers, 1990), 36.
2. Eugene Peterson, "Eat This Book: The Holy Community at Table with the Holy Scripture," *Theology Today* 56 (April 1999): 13–14.
3. Denise Levertov, "The Task," *Oblique Prayers* (New York: New Directions, 1981), 78. Used by permission.
4. Howard E. Gardner, *Frames of Mind: The Theory of Multiple Intelligences* (New York: Basic Books, 1983). Used by permission.
5. Adapted from Norvene Vest, *Gathered in the Word: Praying the Scripture in Small Groups* (Nashville, Tenn.: Upper Room Books, 1996), 9–27.

BIBLE EXPERIENCES FOR YOUNG ADULTS

Method	Description	Kind of Bible Story
Use Art.	Use paint, linoleum block print, markers, clay; illustrate the feeling raised or dominant image or characters of the story.	Visionary stories, words of prophecy, stories with vivid imagery.
Examine the Story's Structure.	Use colored pens, examine words, repetition of phrases, plot line, rhythm, and shared words with other stories.	All stories; particularly helpful with poetry.
Read the Passage in a Variety of Ways.	Read the story using different voices, settings, musical background, inflection, and volume.	Especially effective for longer stories. Also good for very familiar stories.
Act Out the Story.	Act out characters through mime or role-playing or skits focused on the motivations of characters and the feelings raised in roles.	Narrative passages. Skits best used in narratives with dialogue.
Work with Words.	Cut up copy of story and move around phrases; work with synonyms for story's key words.	All stories, but especially treatise passages, letters, arguments.
Write Your Own Words.	Paraphrase story in your own words. Write prayer, parable, song, or litany.	Good for narratives. Match kind of writing to kind of story.
Match Up with a Painting or Poem.	Read and view painting, photo, lithograph, or poem that shares dominant image, theme, or mood with story.	Visionary passage or narrative with dominant images.
Pray or Meditate.	Reflect silently on words, phrases, or images. Stay with the word or phrase and let it conjure up thoughts, feelings, and invitation.	Narratives or visionary passages.
Move.	Identify action words in story and enact them.	Stories that are dominated by particular gesture or movement.
Dialogue with a Character.	Imagine conversation with story's character. Imagine asking questions. Write down imagined responses.	Narratives with strong characters.

1. [ENTERTAINING THE UNEXPECTED

Abraham said, "Let me bring a little bread, that you may refresh yourselves, and after that you may pass on—since you have come to your servant."
Genesis 18:5

> What is hospitality all about? This story of Abraham and Sarah invites us to open ourselves to unexpected guests . . . who may bring more to us than just the dust on their shoes!

LIFE'S A PUSH

EXPECT THE UNEXPECTED

The film *Big Night* (TriStar, 1996; directors, Stanley Tucci and Campbell Scott) features two brothers, Primo and Secondo, struggling to make their livelihood by running a classic Italian restaurant. Of course, like any other hospitality entrepreneurs, they don't know who will walk through their doors next. What separates these brothers from their competition across the street is that they treat each diner with genuine reverence. Each patron is greeted individually. Each customer's request is honored (no matter how unusual). Each meal is prepared with respect and attention to detail and served with affection and genuine interest in the guest's response and enjoyment. The brothers truly honor each and every guest with special care.

In our busy lives, opportunities to host others in our homes may be few and far between. Think about what it takes to extend hospitality to others.

- What do you do to get ready for guests?
- What is it like to anticipate special guests?
- What kind of mood or environment do you try to provide for the people you host?
- How do you convey a sense of welcome to your guests?
- Think about hospitality in terms of expecting the unexpected. Have you ever had anyone "drop in" on you unexpectedly? If this has happened to you, how did it feel? How did you respond? Was the experience an imposition or did you receive any unexpected blessings from it? Would you be ready to receive unexpected guests right now? Why or why not?

25

The Bookers's Open House

The Bookers had often opened up their home in the past. Sometimes, when the children were small, they would even have the children share a bed to give hospitality to someone traveling through. Most weeks they had someone around for a meal after church and had often hosted birthday parties and anniversary parties for people who needed a place to celebrate. But now things were going to be different. Now that two of the children had grown up and left home, it was time to be more intentional. The Bookers decided that from now on they would not simply host people in their home as situations presented themselves. From now on, they would actively look for opportunities to share the good things God had given to them. They would, as far as it was possible, have their two spare rooms full every night with people in need of hospitality.

And so it happened that one night they had a high-profile visiting preacher and a prisoner newly released on parole on the same night. Both left deeply influenced by the other. On another occasion, a woman who worked for a prominent right-wing politician campaigning against legal aid and a woman fleeing an abusive husband shared the same table, and the political aide left with a lot to think about. And, on other occasions, backpackers on their way to new lives, along with old men who'd lived on the street forever, spanned the years in an evening or two.

The Bookers could tell you a hundred stories like this—how they have watched lives change over a warm meal in a safe place or how they have watched their lives change as they have opened themselves to share.

- Imagine yourself as one of the two Booker children living at home or visiting for breaks or vacations. How might you react to all of these different people in your home, at your dinner table, using your bathroom?
- Imagine doing the same thing in your home. What kind of a shift in thinking do you think might be required for you to be as open to hospitality as the Bookers are?
- How do you think the Bookers cope at those times when they don't feel they have the energy left to give?

Servas

Servas International is an organization built around the idea that bringing people together through hospitality is an important way of restoring and maintaining peace in the world. Servas brings together travelers who want to experience life among the people of the places they visit, rather than from the inside of hotels, and hosts who want to offer hospitality and meet and learn from people of different cultures and countries. Begun in 1946, Servas has host families and travelers all across the globe, and over the years many thousands of people from cultures across the world have shared hospitality and, in many cases, begun friendships lasting a lifetime.

Can you imagine a world where potential conflict between two groups of people is averted because the two leaders of each group had become friends across cultures through groups like Servas?

JEAN'S FAMILY

Jean is seventy-one; she has arthritis in one hip and has a fair bit of trouble with her eyes. Even walking down to the shops is pretty much out of the question these days. She gets a little domestic help from the government, but most of her help and support comes from Clive, Nancy, and Russell. Clive, Nancy, and Russell are not related to each other, and they are not related to Jean. They are not rich; in fact, Russell has been in and out of work for years. Sometimes they are not even very easy to get along with—Nancy suffers from severe depression and often talks to no one for days on end. But the three of them are devoted to Jean, and at least one of them visits her every other day.

Jean was a foster parent when she was younger. That meant that she took in children who needed a place to stay in a hurry, sometimes because their parents were sick and had no friends or relatives, sometimes because of abuse or separation or even the death of parents. Some children stayed with Jean a night or two, others for years. Twenty-one children had stayed long enough for Jean to remember them and to still have their photos on the shelf. And now three of these children, who had been welcomed so long ago, are doing what they can to care for the woman who cared for them when no one else would.

Sometimes it seems easy to believe that hospitality is something only for those with the right social skills and money to do. What do you think you actually need to show hospitality to someone?

- Is there anyone in your life to whom you might owe this kind of debt of hospitality and gratitude? Is there anyone who might owe this debt to you?

> **PRAYER**
> Gracious God, may the hospitality we extend to friends and strangers alike be as if we were hosting you—full of generosity and open to unexpected blessings. Amen.

THE STORY

Read Genesis 18:1–15, which follows. Select a way to experience the story found on page 24 or try one of these ideas:

- You might try a multistage meditation on the text, reading it to yourself several times slowly. As you read it the first time, try to visualize the scene like a play unfolding before you. For the second reading, pick a character with whom you identify in some way and experience the story from their perspective. Finally, choose a character that you don't relate to at all and do the same thing. (If you have a tape recorder, try recording yourself reading the story and then use the recording for the meditations.)

- Alternatively, dig out some of the details of the story. If possible, make a photocopy of it so you can mark it up and make notes. In the margin, list the steps involved in receiving a guest (even a stranger). Mark the mentions of haste. Underline the characters who are providing hospitality and circle those who are receiving hospitality. Jot down the characters who are "onstage," but have no speaking roles.

> [1]The Lord appeared to Abraham by the oaks of Mamre, as he sat at the entrance of his tent in the heat of the day. [2]He looked up and saw three men standing near him. When he saw them, he ran from the tent entrance to meet them, and bowed down to the ground. [3]He said, "My lord, if I find favor with you, do not pass by your servant. [4]Let a little water be brought, and wash your feet, and rest yourselves under the tree. [5]Let me bring a little bread, that you may refresh yourselves, and after that you may pass on—since you have come to your servant." So they said, "Do as you have said." [6]And Abraham hastened into the tent to Sarah, and said, "Make ready quickly three measures of choice flour, knead it, and make cakes." [7]Abraham ran to the herd, and took a calf, tender and good, and gave it to the servant, who hastened to prepare it. [8]Then he took curds and milk and the calf that he had prepared, and set it before them; and he stood by them under the tree while they ate.
>
> [9]They said to him, "Where is your wife Sarah?" And he said, "There, in the tent." [10]Then one said, "I will surely return to you in due season, and your wife Sarah shall have a son." And Sarah was listening at the tent entrance behind him. [11]Now Abraham and Sarah were old, advanced in age; it had ceased to be with Sarah after the manner of women. [12]So Sarah laughed to herself, saying, "After I have grown old, and my husband is old, shall I have pleasure?" [13]The Lord said to Abraham, "Why did Sarah laugh, and say, 'Shall I indeed bear a child, now that I am old?' [14]Is anything too wonderful for the Lord? At the set time I will return to you, in due season, and Sarah shall have a son." [15]But Sarah denied, saying, "I did not laugh"; for she was afraid. He said, "Oh yes, you did laugh."

Entertaining the Unexpected 29

YOU PUSH THE STORY

Push the story from Genesis 18 with questions. What about the story unsettles you? What further information would you have wanted for your meditations on the text? Here are some questions with which you might begin and then look to the "Story behind the Story" for further explorations.

PUSH POSSIBILITIES FOR GENESIS 18:1–15
- In their day, what was the significance of the hospitality that Abraham and his household provided to strangers? How does this compare with our understanding of hospitality today?
- Imagine providing hospitality from "behind the scenes" to an honored guest as Sarah is called upon to do. Why did she stay in the tent? What would it feel like to be "heard but not seen?"
- Who are the strangers? How is their identity concealed or revealed?

THE STORY PUSHES YOU

Here's where the story presses on your daily perceptions of your life as it is and how you would like it to be. Some things to think about:

PUSH POSSIBILITIES FOR GENESIS 18:1–15
- Sarah laughed at the promised blessing brought by the guests. How would you have responded? How do you typically respond to promises?
- Sometimes being a host means making yourself somewhat vulnerable. You don't necessarily know what your guests might ask of you. What fears or concerns do you have about extending hospitality to invited guests? to unexpected guests? What sorts of blessings have you received from guests?
- Being a good host includes anticipating needs and meeting them in a gracious and seemingly effortless way. What are some experiences you've had of being hosted well and being a good host yourself?

> ### THE STORY BEHIND THE STORY
> The eastern Mediterranean setting of this story in its time was a rugged environment with few of the travel services and conveniences that we take for granted in our part of the world today. For people traveling by foot, inns or other commercial places to stop just weren't readily available. Most people depended on a cultural code of hospitality in which one gave hospitality freely, while at the same time one could depend on receiving hospitality from others when one needed it in return. This

code of hospitality was not transactional in that one might provide hospitality to one person yet seek it later from another.

Hospitality was the "glue" that held the societies of the Eastern Mediterranean together. In this story, we see two of the most important aspects of the hospitality codes in practice: the roles of host and visitor. Abraham and Sarah, having learned all of the important protocols of hospitality from childhood, play their roles of hosts as they should. Abraham bows to his guests. He formally invites his guests to stay and rest. He offers them the wonderful and precious (remember how dry this country could be) gift of water for them to wash off the dust of the journey. He and Sarah offer them the best food that they are able to provide. In short, Abraham and Sarah do what they are called on to do: They honor these strangers as guests in their home.

These guests also have a role to play within the protocols of hospitality. They are expected to offer a blessing on their hosts and all of their hosts' family group. We as the readers, of course, know that these strangers are no ordinary travelers and that the blessing that they will bring will be no ordinary blessing.

The second part, Genesis 18:9–15, reports the Lord's promise that Sarah would bear a son to Abraham in their old age and Sarah's reaction. Sarah is offstage hearing about the possibility of a son and laughs with incredulity, since she is too old. For a woman in the culture and time of this story, the inability to have a child was seen as a great shame. By contrast, to be able to produce a child, particularly a son to carry on the family line, was considered to be the highest possible achievement for a woman. There is little wonder then that Sarah laughed. Perhaps because she was old and past the age when she could ever hope to produce a child, she had found some peace within herself and had been able to experience her own value as a person beyond her expected role as a mother. Perhaps her laughter was bitter at being valued all her life for only one thing, and that one thing being beyond her power. Perhaps she laughed at the simple absurdity of this situation of three strangers pronouncing such an outlandish blessing! Her laugh provokes the Lord, who makes the promise even clearer—suddenly the laughter turns to fear. She realizes now that she can be heard and that the promise is quite real. The response to Sarah's laughter is not mocking or judging, but is presented as a matter of fact: "Oh yes, you did laugh." God can bring hope to hopeless situations, can give shape to possibilities, and can open the future in a new way.

Entertaining the Unexpected 31

> Hospitality and blessing are inextricably linked in this passage and, indeed, in all of the Scriptures. Think of the way the Gospels talk of Jesus coming into the world as stranger in need of hospitality or all of the blessings he offers to those who share table with him along the course of his ministry. Also, the Sodom and Gomorrah stories that follow our passage are sometimes interpreted as polemics against homosexual orientations. What if we were to read them through the lens of hospitality and blessing? Perhaps their true meaning has to do with the abuse or distortion of these important codes of hospitality.

PUSH OUT

Consider now some of the push-out possibilities listed below:

- Consider working with homeless persons, refugees, or others in need of genuine hospitality. What resource centers exist in your community? Ask a local church pastor or other community leader to help you make connections to such organizations. Are there volunteer opportunities within the organizations that fit your skills and interests and how might you make time in your schedule to participate? Also, you might contact Church World Service at <www.churchworldservice.org> to help you link to a refugee resettlement program in your area or to become involved in their international hospitality efforts. Is there an organization that you're currently affiliated with—perhaps your local church—that you could link to Church World Service in a hospitality project?
- The United Nations declared the year 1999 the "Year of Uprooted and Displaced Peoples." Check out the United Nations Web site at <www.un.org> for links to resources and programs in your area and for more information about this declaration. How might you share it with others?
- You can read more about or join the organization Servas International that was mentioned in the "Life's a Push" section by visiting their Web site at <www.servas.org>.
- Do a culture audit for your area. Visit your local council or city offices for help in determining the cultural makeup of your area. How many languages are spoken? How many people have a language other than English as their first language? How many cultural groups have cultural associations? Are official documents and forms made available in languages other than English? Visit your local school and ask how many languages are spoken in the school. Gather as much information as you can and make a local culture map that can be displayed showing all of the different cultural groups within your area. You might even like to include all of the restaurants of those different cultures on your map!

- Why not draw up a hospitality charter for an organization you're involved with or for a group of friends? It could express how people who come in contact with your organization or group can expect to be welcomed and treated. You could also work on a strategy for how you could go about getting support for your charter from other members to ensure it is adopted and implemented.
- Have a good look at the signs and the doorway of your church building. Do you think the words would make sense to someone who was not familiar with your church? Is it an inviting place to come into? Perhaps you could draw up some plans for signs and entranceways that would really express your church's desire to welcome all.
- In your community—college, organization, church, town, or whatever—it is likely that there are vague territories mapped out in people's heads. This space is where one group hangs out, that room or corner of the yard is for another. Why not do a map that shows where every group gathers and that also shows where those who are by themselves gather? Perhaps you could institute a mini, local Servas International, inviting people from different groups to visit other groups. You never know what might happen!

Entertaining the Unexpected 33

GROUP IDEAS

Focus: To consider the blessings of hospitality and to explore the place of hospitality in the life of faith.

LIFE'S A PUSH

- If possible, invite participants to bring refreshments to share with the group. Set up the space to be as comfortable as possible. Greet group members as they arrive and spend some time just talking and enjoying refreshments before you get started. Think hospitality!
- Ask for volunteers to read the stories "Expect the Unexpected," "The Bookers's Open House," "Servas," and "Jean's Family" to the larger group. Discuss the questions that come with each story.
- Conclude the opening with the prayer on page 27.

THE STORY

- With others, try a role play with parts for the narrator, the visitors (3), Abraham, Sarah, and the servant. As you are going through the role-play, pay special attention to what the readers know as opposed to what the characters know, their staging (onstage or offstage), and their postures.
- Choose a method for your group to experience Genesis 18:1–15 from the selections on page 24.

YOU PUSH THE STORY

- Consider the possibilities to push this story on page 29 and invite participants to come up with their own story pushes.
- As questions arise, find suggested responses in "The Story behind the Story." What questions remain unanswered? How can the group explore them further through research in Bible commentaries or interviewing local scholars or clergy? Do any of the questions lend themselves to more in-depth exploration of a theme or idea—perhaps through a film study or art museum visit?

THE STORY PUSHES YOU

- Discuss the ways we respond to the characters, especially Abraham, Sarah, and God (disguised as a visitor). What ways do they connect to our experience, challenge us, or invite our reflection?
- Engage the push possibilities on page 29, either in small groups or as a whole group. What common themes emerge in the stories of the best experiences of

hospitality given or received? How might these inform a group charter for hospitality? Try creating one together to set the expectations of members and visitors for how they will be treated as part of this group.

Push Out
- Explore the "Push Out" ideas and choose one that you might pursue as a group.

2. [FREEDOM FOR ONE AND FOR ALL

But Moses said to the people, "Do not be afraid, stand firm, and see the deliverance that the Lord will accomplish for you today . . ."

Exodus 14:13a

At times, out of fear, we hold ourselves back from becoming true persons. What courage can we take from the story of God's people at the Red Sea, when they are called to trust rather than fear and to literally march into what God calls them to be?

LIFE'S A PUSH

Hungering to Be Free

Once a hunter spied a flock of quail who were feasting in the tall grass at the edge of the forest. With one swift movement, he had caught them all in his net. He took the birds home and put them in a cage at the back of his house. The poor birds walked around and around the cage, crying and crying. But whenever the man came and tossed in seeds, they greedily pecked them up. All but one bird, that is. There was one bird in the cage who refused to eat and grew thinner and thinner.

At last the day came when the man planned to bring the fattened birds to the market to sell. He looked carefully into the cage, inspecting the quality of his flock. When he noticed the thin bird, he opened the cage and took it out to examine it more closely.

"Why, you're nothing but bones," he said. No sooner had he spoken than the bird flew from his hand to the safety of a branch just out of his reach.

The other birds looked at their free sister and cooed sadly. The free bird sang sadly back, "You ate your captor's food and soon you will die. I refused my captor's food, and now I am free."[1]

Moving away from "captors," like addictions, destructive relationships, confusion about important decisions, or any number of situations that make us feel trapped, can mean setting aside everything familiar, pushing through fear, and believing that things will be better "on the other side." Awakening to social and political forces that prevent life for us and for others can also mean facing fears and believing something better is possible. The personal and the political are not necessarily separate worlds. Movement and becoming in one realm can influence the other. Some things help us march forward towards both greater personal freedom and a better world for all.

COMPANIONS

A person trying to decide about participating in a nonviolent protest against nuclear weapons talks about how his fears were allayed by the presence of experienced others:

> For me, God's call has always felt at first like utter terror . . . a call to forbidden love; a call to a job that I was terrified to take on. But, eventually, I answered those calls. And because of that, ministry came, and "coming out" came, and work in a psychiatric hospital came. But none of that assuaged the initial fears. . . .
>
> We peered through the fence at a spot a quarter-mile away where 1,600 nuclear warheads are stored, knowing that more would be coming—making this the largest assembly of nuclear weapons in the world. We were silent together. We prayed together. And we talked about fear . . . I talked about the fear that brought me there that day. . . . None of us went alone that day. We went accompanied by the strength and presence of others.[2]

FIERCE HOPE

Others push through fear in fierce hope that their community will see better days. Consider the disturbing yet inspiring story of the people of the San Jose de Apartado hamlet of Colombia. This community decided to be an island of nonviolence in the midst of brutality and war. After three years of living out this vision, in spite of all kinds of threats, the village was invaded by armed and hooded men demanding the names of their leaders. Held prisoner, the people insisted they were all leaders and that unarmed neutrality was their defense. The hooded men called them "guerillas." Then one of the Catholic nuns spoke up, testifying to the neutrality of the community. The hooded men grabbed her and threw her down to one side. The gunmen then ordered the women and children to the side threatening to kill them if they didn't comply. Next the armed invaders starting shooting the men of San Jose de Apartado and set the community building on fire. The survivors from the hamlet were forced to move to another location to continue living out their vision of peace and neutrality.[3]

A DEEP MYSTERY
I have a feeling that my boat
has struck, down there in the depths,
against a great thing.
  And nothing
happens! Nothing ... Silence ... Waves ...

—Nothing happens? Or has everything happened,
and are we standing now, quietly, in the new life?[4]

- What kinds of struggles came to mind when you read the story of the quail?
- How do you push through your fears to find freedom from things that hold you back or prevent life?
- Are there some visions of a better world or way of life that are worth risking death?
- Who are the people, principles, and ideals that give you courage and hope?

> **PRAYER**
> Loving God, lead us from death to life, from falsehood to truth, from fear to hope. Amen.

The story of the becoming of the people of Israel depicts God siding with slaves against their Egyptian captors. Experience this summons to faith in a God who calls us out of fear into freedom.

THE STORY
Read the Bible story from Exodus 14. Chose one or more ways to experience this dramatic reading from the list on page 24. Its strong images and action suggest art and drama as possibilities.

> [1]Then the Lord said to Moses: [2]Tell the Israelites to turn back and camp in front of Pi-hahiroth, between Migdol and the sea, in front of Baal-zephon; you shall camp opposite it, by the sea. [3]Pharaoh will say of the Israelites, 'They are wandering aimlessly in the land; the wilderness has closed in on them.' [4]I will harden Pharaoh's heart, and he will pursue them, so that I will gain glory for myself over Pharaoh and all his army;

and the Egyptians shall know that I am the Lord. And they did so. ⁵When the king of Egypt was told that the people had fled, the minds of Pharaoh and his officials were changed toward the people, and they said, "What have we done, letting Israel leave our service?" ⁶So he had his chariot made ready, and took his army with him; ⁷he took six hundred picked chariots and all the other chariots of Egypt with officers over all of them. ⁸The Lord hardened the heart of Pharaoh king of Egypt and he pursued the Israelites, who were going out boldly. ⁹The Egyptians pursued them, all Pharaoh's horses and chariots, his chariot drivers and his army; they overtook them camped by the sea, by Pi-hahiroth, in front of Baal-zephon.

¹⁰As Pharaoh drew near, the Israelites looked back, and there were the Egyptians advancing on them. In great fear the Israelites cried out to the Lord. ¹¹They said to Moses, "Was it because there were no graves in Egypt that you have taken us away to die in the wilderness? What have you done to us, bringing us out of Egypt? ¹²Is this not the very thing we told you in Egypt, 'Let us alone and let us serve the Egyptians'? For it would have been better for us to serve the Egyptians than to die in the wilderness." ¹³But Moses said to the people, "Do not be afraid, stand firm, and see the deliverance that the Lord will accomplish for you today; for the Egyptians whom you see today you shall never see again. ¹⁴The Lord will fight for you, and you have only to keep still."

¹⁵Then the Lord said to Moses, "Why do you cry out to me? Tell the Israelites to go forward. ¹⁶But you lift up your staff, and stretch out your hand over the sea and divide it, that the Israelites may go into the sea on dry ground. ¹⁷Then I will harden the hearts of the Egyptians so that they will go in after them; and so I will gain glory for myself over Pharaoh and all his army, his chariots, and his chariot drivers. ¹⁸And the Egyptians shall know that I am the Lord, when I have gained glory for myself over Pharaoh, his chariots, and his chariot drivers."

¹⁹The angel of God who was going before the Israelite army moved and went behind them; and the pillar of cloud moved from in front of them and took its place behind them. ²⁰It came between the army of Egypt and the army of Israel. And so the cloud was there with the darkness, and it lit up the night; one did not come near the other all night.

²¹Then Moses stretched out his hand over the sea. The Lord drove the sea back by a strong east wind all night, and turned the sea into dry land; and the waters were divided. ²²The Israelites went into the sea on dry ground, the waters forming a wall for them on their right and on

their left. ²³The Egyptians pursued, and went into the sea after them, all of Pharaoh's horses, chariots, and chariot drivers. ²⁴At the morning watch the Lord in the pillar of fire and cloud looked down upon the Egyptian army, and threw the Egyptian army into panic. ²⁵He clogged their chariot wheels so that they turned with difficulty. The Egyptians said, "Let us flee from the Israelites, for the Lord is fighting for them against Egypt."

²⁶Then the Lord said to Moses, "Stretch out your hand over the sea, so that the water may come back upon the Egyptians, upon their chariots and chariot drivers." ²⁷So Moses stretched out his hand over the sea, and at dawn the sea returned to its normal depth. As the Egyptians fled before it, the Lord tossed the Egyptians into the sea. ²⁸The waters returned and covered the chariots and the chariot drivers, the entire army of Pharaoh that had followed them into the sea; not one of them remained. ²⁹But the Israelites walked on dry ground through the sea, the waters forming a wall for them on their right and on their left. ³⁰Thus the Lord saved Israel that day from the Egyptians; and Israel saw the Egyptians dead on the seashore. ³¹Israel saw the great work that the Lord did against the Egyptians. So the people feared the Lord and believed in the Lord and in his servant Moses.

YOU PUSH THE STORY

Press the story with your questions, curiosity, amazement, and frustration. What do you ask of it? Begin with some of the suggestions below. Check out some responses to the questions in "The Story behind the Story" on pages 40–41.

PUSH POSSIBILITIES FOR EXODUS 14:1–31

- Why does God "harden Pharaoh's heart" to pursue the Israelites at the same time as God is trying to free them?
- Is God toying with the Egyptians, "to get glory over Pharaoh?"
- What is the significance of details like the pillar of cloud and the angel switching places?
- Is this a violent, warlike God who takes pleasure in slaughter?
- Are the Israelites truly free once they get to the desert?
- How does this dusty old myth relate to history today? to our lives?
- What are some of your pushes?

THE STORY PUSHES YOU

The radically different world of the story has pushes for us: challenges, visions, and empowerment. Consider some of the following and discover your possibilities.

Push Possibilities for Exodus 14:1–31

- How might the "eleventh hour" doubts and complaints of the Israelites contribute to the authenticity of this story. Do you find it encouraging?
- In what ways are you inspired by the people eventually having enough trust in God to walk through the water?
- What do you think of the image of God as a warrior God destroying the Egyptians? How do you hold together both this image and the image of God as liberator of the people?
- How does the story challenge our contemporary minds? Do you find yourself focusing on investigating the details of how this or that natural wonder actually happened? How do you explore the mystery of faith within or behind those details?
- What does the idea of God taking the side of slaves mean to you?
- In this story, God is seen as transforming public life, the life of whole peoples, in powerful ways. What challenges do you think the story poses to the notion that religion is a private matter separate from politics?
- How else might the story push us?

THE STORY BEHIND THE STORY

This story is the proverbial pebble dropped in the pond, creating ripples through the rest of the Hebrew Scripture for certain and perhaps even the entire Bible. It is the identity-shaping story for the people of Israel. The Christian church inherits this story as well (with due respect to the unique struggles of the Judaic tradition and community). This is a story that shapes the identity of God's people today even as it radically critiques any and all of us who participate in systems that enslave.

This story extends to us an image of ourselves as people formed to trust God even when all the evidence suggests that doubt, fear, and submission ought to be the order of the day. It reminds us that at every point along the way—in the beginning (v. 4), in the middle (v. 18), and at the end (v. 30)—God lets us know who is the Sovereign of creation. It instructs us in the faithful response as God's people. Like the Israelites, we are to fear (be awed by) and believe (v. 31).

The story of crossing the Red Sea is a story of creation. A new people is created. Later in the Hebrew Scripture, the prophets will weave this story together with the story of the creation of the earth in Genesis to remind God's people of who they have been from the beginning (Isaiah 41:20; 43:7, 45:8; 48:7). The images of darkness and wind and the dawning of the day are reminiscent of the creation of the earth when God's Spirit brooded over watery chaos to create (Genesis 1:1–2). God moves and creates in the Exodus story through the pillar of cloud and pillar of fire that move between the Israelites and the Egyptians as a vigilant protective force (14:19–20). God also moves to harden Pharaoh's heart, showing who's really in control of all creation. God can even control the emotion of the ruler of Egypt. In all of this, God is seen as establishing or creating order and protection for slaves and disorder, chaos, and death for the oppressor.

The world of this story suggests that we, as contemporary readers, need to suspend any squeamishness we may have about a God who gloats at the reality of Egyptian horsemen washing up on the shore. We might even have to let go of our questions about how waters were moved around to create a path for the Israelites. Perhaps we have to enter the story at a different level: through the response to a liberating God that it invites. Do not fear. Stand firm. See the deliverance in the hands of God. Be awed by and believe in the One who works on behalf of the oppressed. The call is not for Israel to take up arms but rather for the people to stand firm. If Israel relied on military might, they would be taking on justice themselves and rejecting God's plan. They would be living by the same rules that caused Pharaoh to amass his horses and chariots and riders: an obsession with security and an absence of risk.[5]

PUSH OUT

As we immerse ourselves in the world of pillars of cloud and waters standing up, we encounter the summons to "fear not and stand firm and see . . . " May these suggested "Push Outs" help you to connect with ways to respond to this call.

- The Exodus story is the basis for the Jewish celebration of Passover. Invite someone from the Jewish community to share with a group ways that Passover is celebrated, the symbols it encompasses, and how the story is told within the celebrations.

- The African American community has found great meaning and comfort in the Exodus story as it relates to the experience of slavery in this country. Explore and experience spirituals, stories, and art that interpret Exodus from this perspective.
- Indigenous peoples of North America have asked serious questions about the way many traditions have interpreted the Exodus story because it ends in the uprooting of people indigenous to the land of Palestine. Identify, read, and, perhaps, discuss with a group Native American writings on this topic.
- The story of *The Amistad*, a schooner that in 1839 carried fifty-three Mendi captives from West Africa to be sold into slavery in the United States, is a freedom story. The slaves took over the ship but were later arrested upon reaching the New England shore. Through the efforts of free blacks, abolitionists, and members of churches in the area, their case was defended all the way to the U.S. Supreme Court where they were vindicated and freed to return to their home in Sierra Leone. See the movie *Amistad* and discuss its parallels and contrasts to the Exodus.
- Consider working for peace by becoming involved in one or a number of nonviolent actions across North America that protest some form of oppression or seek some better way of life or greater freedom for all creation. For example, at the time of this writing, there are movements to end the sanctions in Iraq, to close the U.S. Army School of Americas, to protest improper storage of depleted uranium, and to speak out against the U.S. military participation in Colombia. Join with those who are sharing information and planning public witness. Talk about your fears in participating in these movements. Talk about the things that help you risk doing something that may bring controversy and rejection, even arrest, on behalf of your hopes and visions for a better day. The national organization Peace Action has a Web site <www.peaceaction.org> with lots of good ideas.
- Edgar Allan Poe wrote a story, "Descent into the Maelstrom," that details two different responses to the fear of destruction and death. Find it in *The Complete Stories and Poems of Edgar Allan Poe* (Garden City, N.Y.: Doubleday, 1996). Read it and discuss the way we experience fear in times of crisis, or change.
- Do you have a freedom story? Have you ever found yourself living through fear and standing firm in a goal, a belief, or simply life itself? Consider writing your story, illustrating it artistically, or sharing it with others in some other way.

GROUP IDEAS

[Focus: To encounter the summons from God to move out of fear into freedom.

LIFE'S A PUSH
- Begin by inviting participants to define "freedom" and "liberation." Record the definitions on newsprint.
- Read aloud one or more of the vignettes on pages 35–37.
- Raise some of the questions in "Life's a Push" for discussion.
- Offer the prayer that can be found on page 37 or one of yours.

THE STORY
- Have multiple voices read aloud the story from Exodus 14.
- Invite a time of silence for participants to sit with the story after the reading.
- Select a way of experiencing the story from the list on page 24. Consider matching the story with paintings or poems that reflect its themes or images. Paintings by artist Jacob Lawrence might be particularly appropriate, if those are available to you through an Internet search or library.

YOU PUSH THE STORY
- Begin by raising some of the push possibilities on page 39.
- Ask participants to add their pushes.
- Turn together to "The Story behind the Story" on pages 40–41 and look for possible responses to some of these questions.

THE STORY PUSHES YOU
- Ask participants what is important about this story for them and for the world. If earlier you recorded definitions of "freedom" and "liberation" on the newsprint, make notes about the significance of this passage on the same page.
- Look together at other push possibilities on page 40.

PUSH OUT
- Select one or more of the "Push Outs" and have resources ready for the group to engage in the selection.
- Evaluate how well the "Push Out" helped the group address this session's focus on freedom and moving through fear, both personally and politically.
- Invite the group to consider other "Push Outs."
- Offer the prayer below or one of yours.

> **PRAYER**
> We offer up our fears to you, O God, that we might go forward with trust in you to new freedom and a better day for all. Amen.

1. Elisa Davy Pearmain, ed., *Doorways to the Soul: 52 Wisdom Tales from around the World* (Cleveland: Pilgrim Press, 1998), 49.
2. Peter Ilgenfritz, "Beyond Fear," *The Other Side* 36, no. 4 (July/August 2000): 32–33.
3. Jackie Downing and John Hickman, eds., "Massacre at the Peace Community," *Action on Colombia, Columbia Support Network* (summer 2000): 7.
4. Juan Ramon Jimenez, "Oceans," *News of the Universe: Poems of Twofold Consciousness*, ed. and trans. Robert Bly (San Francisco: Sierra Club Books, 1980), 105. Used by permission.
5. J. P. M. Walsh, *The Mighty from Their Thrones: Power in the Biblical Tradition* (Philadelphia: Fortress Press, 1987), 68.

3. [BATTLE OF THE SEXES

And she said, "I will surely go with you; nevertheless, the road on which you are going will not lead to your glory, for the Lord will sell Sisera into the hand of a woman." Then Deborah got up and went with Barak to Kedesh.

Judges 4:9

> Women and men together bear the pain of the oppression of women through violence, suspicion, and the denial of their full humanity. We push the story of a strong female character in the Bible to help us bring peace to the battle of the sexes.

LIFE'S A PUSH

LAMENT IN THE HEADLINES

Just a single day's newspaper headlines are enough to express the deep, painful, and ongoing struggles women and men often experience in relating to one another as friends, intimate partners, colleagues, and members of the human race. Today's stories? The Worldwide Wrestling Federation is trying to convince the two female finalists from TV's *Survivor* to settle their bitter differences in the wrestling ring. The male winner of *Survivor*, meanwhile, is resting easy with a cool million. A city councilor of a mid-sized city is celebrated as the first public official in the region to give birth to a child during the term of her office. A government campaign in Thailand posts signs on city streets warning that women who wear skirts with a hem above the knee are inviting sexual violence. A lawsuit charges that men working on an auto assembly line at a major auto manufacturer felt free to grope women or ask them to bare their breasts while on the job. A new book details the icy, abusive relationship of a former U.S. president towards his wife.

Reading all of this, we realize that we carry a legacy of struggle, hurt, and confusion between the sexes—and between and among people in general—in our hearts, our words, and our actions. Women point fingers at men. Men point fingers at women. Politicians point fingers at families. Citizens point fingers at politicians. Religion points fingers at culture. Culture points fingers at religion. Aside from placing blame, we are left with a longing for healing, for new ways of seeing, and for a sense of right relationship.

MISEDUCATION
Singer Lauryn Hill laments the struggle of intimate relationship in the song "Ex-Factor."

> It could all be so simple, but you'd rather make it hard
> Loving you is like a battle and we both end up with scars
> Tell me, who I have to be to get some reciprocity
> No one loved you more than me and no one ever will
>
> Is this just a silly game that forces you to act this way
> Forces you to scream my name then pretend that you can't stay
> Tell me, who I have to be to get some reciprocity
> No one loves you more than me and no one ever will.[1]

What role has religion played in our education, or, perhaps better, our miseducation about gender, sex, and power? The wife of a missionary preacher to the Congo raises this painful question in Barbara Kingsolver's book, *The Poisonwood Bible*:

> I'm not the first woman on earth to have seen her daughters possessed. For time and eternity there have been fathers . . . who simply can see no way to have a daughter but to own her like a plot of land. To work her, plow her under, rain down a dreadful poison upon her. . . . I'd come to believe that God was on his side. Does this make me some lunatic? But I did believe it; I must have. I feared him more than it's possible to fear a mere man. Feared Him, loved Him, served Him, clamped my hands over my ears to stop His words that rang in my head even when He was far away, or sleeping.[2]

VICIOUS CYCLE
It is not just women who suffer in this human struggle of relationship, but men as well. In an extreme example, a male character played by Tom Cruise in the movie *Magnolia* (New Line Productions, 1999; director, Paul Thomas Anderson) builds an entire workshop for other men on how to "seduce and destroy" women. Deeply hurt when his father abandons him, leaving him to take care of his terminally ill mother until her death, his response is to perpetuate the pain.

Author Sam Keen speaks to the angst of intimacy between women and men from the male perspective:

The average man spends a lifetime denying, defending against, trying to control, and reacting to the power of WOMAN. . . . We have invested so much of our identity, committed so much of our energy, and squandered so much of our power in trying to control, avoid, conquer, or demean women because we are so vulnerable to their mysterious power over us. Like sandy atolls in a monsoon-swept ocean, the male psyche is in continual danger of being inundated by the feminine sea.[3]

- How do you respond to these examples of the struggles of human relationships?
- What are some things that come to mind when you think about the impact of gender roles and expected norms for each sex on relationships between men and women? among people in general?
- What role, if any, do you think religion plays in shaping our understanding of these roles?
- Do you think, as Sam Keen suggests, that men spend a lot of energy protecting themselves from "the power of woman"? Why or why not?

> **PRAYER**
> Tender God, touch us, be touched by us,
> Make us lovers of humanity, compassionate friends of all creation.
> Gracious God, hear us into speech, speak us into acting,
> and through us, recreate the world.[4]

A woman leader of Israel, Deborah, and a male general, Barak, are characters in a story that helps us look at the portrayal of men and women in the Bible and explore our own understandings and assumptions about gender-specific roles in family, politics, and culture.

THE STORY

Read the Bible story from Judges 4. Then choose one or more ways to experience the story from the list on page 24.

THE STORY

[4] At that time Deborah, a prophetess, wife of Lappidoth, was judging Israel. [5] She used to sit under the palm of Deborah between Ramah and Bethel in the hill country of Ephraim; and the Israelites came up to her for judgment. [6] She sent and summoned Barak son of Abinoam from Kedesh in Naphtali, and said to him, "The Lord, the God of Israel, commands you, 'Go, take position at Mount Tabor, bringing ten thousand from the tribe of Naphtali and the tribe of Zebulun. [7] I will draw out Sisera, the general of Jabin's army, to meet you by the Wadi Kishon with his chariots and his troops; and I will give him into your hand.'" [8] Barak said to her, "If you will go with me, I will go; but if you will not go with me, I will not go." [9] And she said, "I will surely go with you; nevertheless, the road on which you are going will not lead to your glory, for the Lord will sell Sisera into the hand of a woman." Then Deborah got up and went with Barak to Kedesh. [10] Barak summoned Zebulun and Naphtali to Kedesh; and ten thousand warriors went up behind him; and Deborah went up with him. . . .

[14] Then Deborah said to Barak, "Up! For this is the day on which the Lord has given Sisera into your hand. The Lord is indeed going out before you." So Barak went down from Mount Tabor with ten thousand warriors following him. [15] And the Lord threw Sisera and all his chariots and all his army into a panic before Barak; Sisera got down from his chariot and fled away on foot. . . . [16] All the army of Sisera fell by the sword; no one was left.

[17] Now Sisera had fled away on foot to the tent of Jael wife of Heber the Kenite; for there was peace between King Jabin of Hazor and the clan of Heber the Kenite. [18] Jael came out to meet Sisera, and said to him, "Turn aside, my lord, turn aside to me; have no fear." So he turned aside to her into the tent, and she covered him with a rug. [19] Then he said to her, "Please give me a little water to drink; for I am thirsty." So she opened a skin of milk and gave him a drink and covered him. [20] He said to her, "Stand at the entrance of the tent, and if anybody comes and asks you, 'Is anyone here?' say, 'No.'" [21] But Jael wife of Heber took a tent peg, and took a hammer in her hand, and went softly to him and drove the peg into his temple, until it went down into the ground—he was lying fast asleep from weariness—and he died. [22] Then, as Barak came in pursuit of Sisera, Jael went out to meet him, and said to him, "Come, and I will show you the man whom you are seeking." So we went into her tent and there was Sisera lying dead, with the tent peg in his temple.

Battle of the Sexes 49

YOU PUSH THE STORY

Bring to this story your confusion, hope, anger, or curiosity, especially with regard to the portrayal of female and male characters and the character of God. Here are some suggested questions to get you started. Explore these questions and others you may have in conversation with the "Story behind the Story" on pages 50–51.

PUSH POSSIBILITIES FOR JUDGES 4:4–10, 14–22

- Who are the judges and why is Deborah called a "judge"? How does she compare with other judges in the book of Judges?
- How is the warrior God of Israel different from the gods of the Canaanites?
- Why does Barak ask Deborah if she will go with him into battle? Is he afraid? Does he need her presence? Does he distrust her?
- What do you think it means that Deborah is sometimes referred to as the "Mother of Israel"?
- Why do the Israelites have to fight the army of Sisera?
- Whose side is Jael on? Is she the hero or heroine of the story?
- Are the women in the story portrayed as being different from the men? If you think so, how are they different?

THE STORY PUSHES YOU

Allow the story to push back in ways that might judge, heal, or offer insight into the ways we see God and one another today. Consider the push possibilities below.

PUSH POSSIBILITIES FOR JUDGES 4:4–10, 14–22

- How does the image of God going to war on Israel's behalf support or challenge other ways of thinking about God? Is this the God you know and love or are other images more central to your faith and understanding?
- Are the people against whom the Israelites fight simply evil or might they also be victims in the story?
- Do you believe that God uses non-Israelites like Jael for divine purposes?
- How have images of God in the Bible been influenced by cultural understandings of human beings, and how have cultural understandings of human beings been influenced by images of God in the Bible?

THE STORY BEHIND THE STORY
The backdrop to the story of the Judges is Israel's painful process of seeking national unity among all of its tribes. It comes out of a time of military emergency after the initial "conquest" of the Promised Land. There is a cycle to the whole book of Judges. The Israelites do evil; God sells them into the hands of the enemy; Israel cries out for God's help; and, finally, God raises a judge or ruler to deliver them. The later judges become more and more unfaithful and ineffectual to the point where Israel raises up a king to unify the nation. Deborah is the only "judge" who does more than go to war. She is remembered as a great ruler because she also mediates disputes between the people.

According to the book of Judges, the God of Israel is a warrior god fighting on behalf of a nomadic people against the Canaanite gods of agriculture and technology. The iron chariots of Sisera's army are no match against this God who acts to save a wandering people commanded not to believe in the idols of fertility and seasons.

Under Deborah, God hears the cries of the Israelites who had been cruelly oppressed for twenty years by the King of Canaan (Judges 4:2–3). Jael's people, the people of the hammer, had alliances with both Israel and Canaan.

There are lots of possible reasons for Barak to ask Deborah to go into battle with him. Maybe he thinks she represents the presence of God. Maybe he doesn't trust her judgment because she had a military track record. Maybe he is a coward. In any case, Deborah is portrayed as the mother of Israel (5:7) in the famous Song of Deborah that follows this passage with Barak. She is compared to the mother of Sisera, waiting for his return at the window and assuming he is delayed because he is dividing the spoils of war and raping the women of Israel. Sisera's mother is assured that he will bring back some fashionable clothing for her (5:28–31). Hardly a noble yearning.

God raises up the outsider Jael to assure the victory for the Israelites and to prevent the women of Israel from being raped and ravaged by Sisera's army. We might assume that the army of Israel would do the same to the Canaanite women. (See Deuteronomy 21:10–14). Jael breaks all the rules of hospitality by killing Sisera! She is portrayed as "mothering Sisera to death" by covering him, offering him milk when he asks for water, and letting him take a nap.[5] Like Delilah, whose story is told later in Judges (16:4–22), she is portrayed as seducing men.[6] In Judges, men kill men in battle, and they are heroes. Women kill men by seduction or deception (Jael and Delilah) or because they send their sons to war as the mother of Israel (Deborah). Men kill their own daughters as sacrifice (11:39) or concubines for almost no reason at all (19:29). All in all, women are portrayed as idealized mothers, seductresses who cannot be trusted, or virgins and concubines with little or no worth.

Perhaps Israel is not on "the right side." Perhaps the real battle is not a triumph over the Canaanites, their religion, or even their technology, but a triumph of male warrior ideas. Perhaps Deborah is the character and mouthpiece (in the Song of Deborah) of the male ideas of war, pillage, and rape.[7] Perhaps the God of Judges uses women as bit players in a drama where men gain power by war, domestic violence, and pillage.[8]

PUSH OUT

The pictures of God and God's people in the story clash with many of our understandings today. Our challenge is to see the Biblical story as a vehicle to faith in the midst of that clash and experience a growth in our perspective. Here are some suggested "Push Outs" to continue the struggle to find healthy identities as women and men:

- Spend more time with the Bible and read how it portrays women. Read the Song of Deborah in Judges 5, the story of Samson and Delilah in Judges 16. Look at the story of Tamar in 2 Samuel 13 or the story of Ruth. Don't rule out stories of the New Testament, such as the hemorrhaging woman (Mark 5:24–34), the Syrophonecian woman (Matthew 15:21–28, Mark 7:24–30), the woman who anoints Jesus (Mark 14:3–9), 1 Timothy 4–5, or Paul's words about Hagar and Sarah (Galatians 4:21–31). Discuss these portrayals and what they mean for the church today as we read the Bible. *Bad Girls of the Bible* (Cleveland: The Pilgrim Press, 1999) by Barbara J. Essex and Linda H. Hollies's book, *Jesus and Those Bodacious Women* (Cleveland: The Pilgrim Press, 1998), are good places to start.
- Watch the video *Holy Smoke* (Miramax Films, 2000; director: Jane Campion) about a young woman who is drawn into an ashram in India and is encouraged by her family to be desensitized on retreat with an American cult expert. Discuss how the relationship between religion and sexuality is portrayed in the movie. How can religious authority be used as power over others?

- Get to know the issues of domestic violence and other forms of sexual violence. Work with a clergyperson or trained professional to create a retreat with staff from a local domestic violence shelter, rape crisis center, or a trained counselor who works with survivors of sexual abuse, rape, and domestic violence to educate your community about theses issues and ways to help prevent them. Be aware that there may be persons in your group who are survivors and who will need an opportunity to have an immediate confidential referral to a qualified professional. The Feminist Majority Foundation has a "Violence against Women" Web site with lots of local resource links at <www.feminist.org>.
- Collect newspaper articles, comic strips, TV images, advertisements, and billboard images to create a collage or collages that portray women and men a various roles of leader, parent, sexual being, colleague, friend, and child. Discuss what you find.
- Seek opportunities for men to explore issues of male spirituality. Richard Rohr, a Franciscan priest, has an audiotape series, *A Man's Approach to God* (St. Anthony Messenger Press; 1615 Republic Street; Cincinnati, Ohio 45210; 513-241-5615). Frank Leib's book, *Friendly Competitors, Fierce Companions* (Cleveland: The Pilgrim Press, 1997), William O. Roberts Jr.'s book *Crossing the Soul's River* (Cleveland: The Pilgrim Press, 1998), and Stephen Boyd's book, *The Men We Long to Be* (Cleveland: The Pilgrim Press, 1997) are helpful resources.
- Do a survey of current music. Listen to a collection of songs and review the lyrics and liner notes. What messages do the songs give about gender roles and relations between men and women? Lauryn Hill's "Ex-Factor" on the CD *The Mideduction of Lauryn Hill* (Columbia Records, 1998) is especially poignant.

Battle of the Sexes

GROUP IDEAS

[Focus: To explore some of the wonderful ways the Bible explodes our cultural understandings of gender roles.

LIFE'S A PUSH
- Select one or more vignettes on pages 45–47 and read them aloud. Include a clip from the film *Magnolia* if you have access to it and have time.
- Spend time with the questions included in "Life's a Push" on page 47.
- Offer the prayer included.

THE STORY
- Have copies of the story available so participants can each read it. Then ask someone to read it aloud.
- Chose a method or methods with which to experience the story from the suggestions on page 24. A dialogue with the characters or guided meditation may be helpful methods.

YOU PUSH THE STORY
- Invite participants to raise questions of the story. Have someone write them down.
- Suggest pushes included on page 49.
- Together read "The Story behind the Story" on pages 50–51 aloud and discuss it.

THE STORY PUSHES YOU
- Ask participants for ways the story heals, judges, or offers new insight.
- Look together at the push possibilities listed on page 49.

PUSH OUT
- Prepare a "Push Out" activity from those suggested and have a resource or resources ready.
- Invite the group to consider ways to continue to push out from the story, including the list provided on pages 51–52.
- Offer the closing prayer below or one of yours.

> **PRAYER**
> Male and female, you created us in your image, God. May we grow in that image as we hear one another's stories, claim our own stories, and struggle with the Bible story. Amen.

1. Lauryn Hill, "Ex-Factor," *The Miseduction of Lauryn Hill*, CD (Columbia Records, 1998). Used by permission.
2. Barbara Kingsolver, *The Poisonwood Bible* (New York: HarperPerennial, 1998), 191–92. Used by permission.
3. Sam Keen, *Fire in the Belly: On Being a Man*, (New York: Bantam, 1991); qtd. in Allan G. Johnson, *The Gender Knot: Unraveling Our Patriarchal Legacy* (Philadelphia: Temple University Press, 1997), 200.
4. Carter Heyward, "Blessing," *Celebrating Women*, ed. Hannah Ward, Jennifer Wild, and Janet Morley (London: Women in Theology; Movement for the Ordination of Women, 1986), 39. Used by permission of SPCK.
5. Danna Nolan Fewell and David M. Gunn, *Gender, Power, and Promise: The Subject of the Bible's First Story* (Nashville, Tenn.: Abingdon, 1993), 122–27. Used by permission.
6. Mieke Bal, *Death and Dissymmetry: The Politics of Coherence in the Book of Judges* (Chicago: University of Chicago Press, 1988), 206–17; and *Murder and Difference: Gender, Genre and Scholarship on Sisera's Death*, trans. Matthew Gumpert (Bloomington, Ind.: Indiana University Press, 1988), 44–46.
7. Gale A. Yee, ed., *Judges and Method* (Minneapolis: Augsburg Fortress Press, 1995), 70–75.
8. Carole Fontaine, "The Abusive Bible: On Use of Feminist Method in Pastoral Context," *A Feminist Companion to Reading the Bible: Approaches, Methods, and Strategies*, ed. Athalya Brenner (Sheffield, England: Sheffield Academic Press, 1997), 98.

4. [LIVING THE HARD QUESTIONS

> He still persists in his integrity, although you incited me against him, to destroy him for no reason.
> Job 2:3c

> When we are suffering, we cry out for some kind of response: answers, help, and reassurance. Job's response from God is the assurance that he suffers not because of God, but with God.

LIFE'S A PUSH

Why people suffer through no fault of their own remains one of the most stubborn questions of all time. How we respond to the question of suffering says a lot about how we understand the world, God, and ourselves. Even as we work to understand suffering and somehow make sense of it, we also recognize that, at a certain level, all words and theories ring hollow when we come face-to-face with loss of life, or heartbreak, or pain.

We also know that many religions have addressed the issue of suffering in ways that have only heaped more pain and confusion onto those in the thick of tragedy or difficulty. Such harmful misinterpretations have caused people to question the role and validity of religious responses altogether.

Just consider what you may have heard religious folk say about suffering. Some say it's punishment. Others say God has abandoned us. Others decide that God has neither the capacity nor the inclination to do anything about it.

SUE GOD?

A character with AIDS in Tony Kushner's famous play, *Angels in America*, perhaps speaks for many when he rages against the belief that God would just leave the earth alone to its own devices. Prior (the character) addresses a council in heaven comprised of representatives from each of the world's continents. Near the end of the second part of the play, Prior acts as though he puts God on trial:

Prior: God . . .

(Thunderclap)

Prior: He isn't coming back. And even if He did. . . . If He ever did come back, if He ever dared to show His face, or his Glyph, or whatever in the Garden again . . . if after all this destruction, if after all the terrible days of this terrible century he returned to see . . . how much suffering His abandonment had created, if all He has to offer is death, you should sue the bastard. That's my only contribution to all this Theology. Sue the bastard for walking out. How dare He.[1]

- Have you ever wanted to say something like that to God or one of God's defenders?
- What alternatives are there to thinking that God has abandoned the world?
- How do we know if God responds at all?

AWAKING TO PURPOSE

I have a friend who was in so much anguish from depression that she took a bottle of powerful pills one Thanksgiving weekend. For a month afterward, she lay in intensive care while her family tried to decide whether or not to take her off the life-support systems. No one expected her to live. But then she took a turn for the better and, gradually, she regained all of her faculties. At one point in her recovery, she raged at God, "Why did you let me live?" Months later, when I visited her, her questions were very different. Still in physical pain, still requiring lots of medicine for depression, she now asks questions like, "Okay, God, what is it that you want me to do?" and "How can I come to know what purposes you have for my life?"

- Our questions for God often change as we live through them. Does this story remind you of changes in the questions you're living?
- How do you react to what happened in this woman's life and in her thinking?

> **PRAYER**
> God, we thank you for the chance to ask hard questions. In the questioning and the calling for your response, may we find some peace, a sense of your presence, and a bond with one another. Amen.

Living the Hard Questions 57

We all ask "big" questions about what it all means, especially in times of crisis. We want some answers—or at least some kind of response. The biblical character Job goes through things that make him raise many questions. He doesn't get any answers, but he does hear from God.

THE STORY

Read the Bible story from Job. If time allows, read more of the book of Job, which stands as one complete story. Choose a way to experience the story from the ideas found on page 24.

> 1:1 There was once a man in the land of Uz whose name was Job. That man was blameless and upright, one who feared God and turned away from evil.
>
> 2:1 One day the heavenly beings came to present themselves before the Lord, and Satan also came among them to present himself before the Lord. ²The Lord said to Satan, "Where have you come from?" Satan answered the Lord, "From going to and fro on the earth, and from walking up and down on it." ³The Lord said to Satan, "Have you considered my servant Job? There is no one like him on the earth, a blameless and upright man who fears God and turns away from evil. He still persists in his integrity, although you incited me against him, to destroy him for no reason. ⁴Then Satan answered the Lord, "Skin for skin! All that people have they will give to save their lives. ⁵But stretch out your hand now and touch his bone and flesh, and he will curse you to your face." ⁶The Lord said to Satan, "Very well, he is in your power; only spare his life."
>
> ⁷So Satan went out from the presence of the Lord, and inflicted loathsome sores on Job from the sole of his foot to the crown of his head. ⁸Job took a potsherd with which to scrape himself, and sat among the ashes.
>
> ⁹Then his wife said to him, "Do you still persist in your integrity? Curse God, and die." ¹⁰But he said to her, "You speak as any foolish woman would speak. Shall we receive the good at the hand of God, and not receive the bad?" In all this Job did not sin with his lips.

YOU PUSH THE STORY

Press the opening of Job's dramatic story with your questions and challenges. What is difficult to understand? What's missing? What is unbelievable? What is intriguing? Look in the "Story behind the Story" section on pages 58–60 for possible responses to the questions below and others you may have.

Push Possibilities for Job 1:1; 2:1–10

- What sort of arrangement does there seem to be between God and Satan? Is God bargaining with people's lives?
- Who is Satan?
- Does evil come at the hands of God?
- Does cursing God really mean death, as Job's wife suggests?
- Why does Job suffer if he hasn't done anything wrong?
- What happens next in the story? Does Job survive the struggle?
- Why is Job's wife called "foolish"?

THE STORY PUSHES YOU

Make room for the story to bring you consolation, hope, challenge, or new perspective. How does this story confirm or expand your understanding of suffering and God's response to it?

Push Possibilities for Job 1:1; 2:1–10

- How might the story of Job suggest a different response to the question, "Why do bad things happen to good people?"
- What does the story suggest about "faithful" conduct for someone who suffers?
- How do we see prayer at work in this story?
- Is God both all-powerful and all-loving?
- Does faith in God depend on things going well for us?
- Is it worse to suffer without answers to the question "why" or to suffer without God?

THE STORY BEHIND THE STORY

What's included in the chapter discussed here is merely an opening glimpse of this great story of Job. In the first chapter, Satan suggests to God that the reason Job is so blameless and faithful is because God has offered him so many blessings. Job is rich, healthy, happily married, and has ten children and lots of animals and servants. To test this premise, God gives Satan permission to take away Job's servants, oxen, donkeys, and camels, and all of his children are put to death. As we have read, God allows Satan to actually persecute Job's own body.

Three of Job's friends come and sit with him for an entire week without saying anything. Finally, a poem begins in chapter 3, and Job lets out a cry. Stephen Mitchell's translation of Job 3:3 has Job crying, "God damn the day I was born and the night that forced me from the womb.

Why couldn't I have died as they pulled me out of the dark?"[2]

For thirty-seven chapters, Job defends his innocence. Eventually his friends turn against Job when he starts accusing God of injustice (16, 19, 21). They pick through the evidence of his life, looking for a reason for this suffering. He must have deserved it, they begin to claim, because it can't be God's fault. The friends come up with all kinds of lofty theories about why this is happening to Job, all the religious responses, perhaps, that we have all heard at one time or another. The more Job cries out, the more they build their theories. The friends argue from wisdom, from tradition, from religious sayings, and from universally held ideas. Job denies all the common sense, all the traditions and rational arguments, and stands by his claim, "I am not guilty!" And, in drawing conclusions in this logic, Job seems to say, "God has done me wrong."

Toward the end (29—31), we hear Job no longer addressing his friends, but talking directly to God. With his back up against the dung heap on which he sits, Job yells to God about all the ways he is blameless and demands, "Why is this happening to me? God, answer me!"

Then God does speak to Job, out of a whirlwind. God says, "Who is this that darkens counsel by words without knowledge? Gird up your loins like a man, I will question you, and you shall declare to me. Where were you when I laid the foundations of the earth?" (38:2–4) Then, as Jewish scholar Lawrence Kushner says, God shows Job the *Mutual of Omaha's Wild Kingdom* video of lions ripping apart gazelles, vultures swooping down on carrion, and all the other messy things of creation and says to Job, "What do you think of that? I'm in that too!"[3] For four chapters, God tells Job that he has no idea of the mystery of God, but never answers Job's question. Job asked about justice. God talks in the whirlwind about creative power and mystery beyond human understanding.[4]

Eventually, Job concedes. In a sense, Job tells God he was talking about stuff about which he had no clue (42). "I had heard of you by the hearing of the ear, but now my eye sees you" (v. 5), says Job. Job then repents before God. The story closes with Job's fortunes and health restored by God.

This story might be seen as a response to the understanding of God's retribution that we read about in other places in the Hebrew Scripture and, perhaps, prominent during the time the book was written. Retribution says, "If I do something wrong, God will punish me for it." Kind of like those billboards many of us see on highways these days that say things like, "Curse me and I'll make rush hour longer.—God." Job's friends, in many ways, represent this traditional way of thinking.

> But even Job's understanding turns out to be inadequate in this story. It is not enough to stand by his blamelessness and, therefore, say that God must be to blame. In the whirlwind, it becomes very clear that God is much greater than blame and legal categories.
>
> Satan in the story is not the devil, but a respectable member of God's cabinet, who acts as God's prosecutor. His name in Hebrew is *Ha-Satan*, "the Accuser," and it is his job to bring people to trial, but only when God says so.
>
> Job's wife can be considered foolish if you only have two choices: to be right and innocent or to be wrong and suffer God's wrath. But Job finds out in the end that those are not the only choices. To see God face-to-face and to know God's presence is perhaps the only response there is to suffering. Perhaps knowing that presence is profoundly more important than knowing the answer to "why?"

PUSH OUT

The drama of Job is a powerful vessel for our own grappling with hard questions of faith. Consider ways to deepen the experience of God coming in a whirlwind to our demanding cries and questions on our own dung heaps as we scrape away at our own sores of life.

- Read the book of Job in its entirety and continue its discussion. Consider reading Stephen Mitchell's *The Book of Job* (San Francisco: North Point Press, 1979).
- View the movie *Life is Beautiful* (Miramax Films, 1998; director Roberto Benigni) and discuss the ways that life and love and a "presence" is celebrated even in the grimmest of circumstances.
- Explore ways people of faith can respond to people who suffer with mental illness and their families. Many denominations have passed resolutions on mental illness and the church's response. The National Alliance for the Mentally Ill; 1901 North Fort Myer Drive, Suite 500; Arlington, Virginia 22209; <www.NAMI.org> is one resource. They have produced the videotape, "A Place to Come Home To—Chronic Mental Illness and the Church."
- Volunteer with your local hospice care program, AIDS hospice, or other organization that provides care and support for persons with terminal illness and their families. Keep an open posture as you accompany persons who ask hard questions as they suffer.

- Read Mark Slouka's essay, "Blood on the Tracks: Does Senseless Death Reveal God or His Absence?" in *Harper's: Celebrating 150 Years of Literature* about a train accident in May 1999. In the essay, Slouka writes about our information age, "Necessity and absence are giving birth to something new: a bloodier God, or a truer silence."[5] Discuss how the immediacy of tragedy across the globe deluges us and how that impacts the way we view God's role in undeserved suffering.

GROUP IDEAS

Focus: To tackle the difficult question of undeserved suffering, guided by the story of Job.

Life's a Push
- Have Bibles, copies of "The Story," and "Push Possibilities" available in the gathering space. You may have a newspaper clipping of a recent story from local or global news that raises lots of questions about God's participation in tragedy. You may choose to spend some time talking about people's reactions to that news.
- Ask individual participants to read aloud "Sue God?" and "What Do You Want Me to Do?" and engage in discussion using the questions on page 56 or other questions you may have.
- Offer the prayer on page 56 or one of yours.

The Story
- Ask participants to read silently the story from Job. Then invite three people to read it aloud, using different voices for narrator, God, and Satan.
- Choose a way to experience the story from suggestions on page 24. Since only a small portion of this story is actually included in the session, you may choose to find ways to let the group get to know more of the story of Job. Perhaps someone could be prepared with a summary. The imagery of the heavenly court, the dung heap, the friends, and the whirlwind are all quite powerful. Choose methods that will help visualize the scenes of the story.

You Push the Story
- Pass out copies of "You Push the Story" on pages 57–58. Invite the participants to look over the possibilities and write down additional pushes they may have.
- Open discussion with participants sharing their push preferences. Look together at "The Story behind the Story" for possible responses. Ask the participants for ideas of other possible responses.

The Story Pushes You
- List together possible ways the story challenges, heals, or gives new perspective. As a guide, refer to the list provided on page 58.
- Spend some time discussing one or more of the pushes.

Push Out

- Select together one or more of the "Push Out" experiences or begin planning for one of them at your next gathering.
- Offer the prayer below or one of yours.

> **PRAYER**
>
> Creator and Holy Visitor, give us senses to receive your appearances to us and your response of abiding with us in our questions and our suffering. Amen.

---

1. Tony Kushner, *Angels in America: A Gay Fantasia on National Themes. Part Two: Perestroika* (New York: Theatre Communications Group, 1992), 130. Used by permission.
2. Stephen Mitchell, *Into the Whirlwind: A Translation of the Book of Job* (Garden City, N.Y.: Doubleday, 1979), 13.
3. Lawrence Kushner, "An Ocean of God: Neo-Cabalistic Reflections on the Inner-Connectedness of All-Being," Trinity Parish Institute 31st Annual Conference (New York: Trinity Television, 2000).
4. Barbara Brown Taylor, *Home by Another Way* (Cambridge: Cowley, 1999), 165.
5. Mark Slouka, "Blood on the Tracks: Does Senseless Death Reveal God or His Absence?" *Harper's Magazine* 300, no. 1801 (June 2000): 96.

5. ["I WILL BE WITH YOU"

I have called you by name, you are mine.
Isaiah 43:1b

In a time of distress and suffering, the people of God received a message of comfort and presence. Are you ready to be embraced by unconditional love and commitment?

LIFE'S A PUSH

Are there days when you feel cut off from the world and everyone in it, even though you are surrounded by people and busy with all the usual things? What's going on with you when that happens? Is it the pain of missing a loved one, a relative, or someone else you're close to? Is it being overwhelmed by the sheer volume of everything life throws at you and the feeling that none of it seems to mean anything? Do you ever feel lonely in a crowd?

When I find myself in an aloneness funk, I pull out familiar and favorite CDs. I'm not looking for a new experience or a new message, but rather something more reassuring, deeper, and safer. There are certain songs in which I find imprints of powerful longing, faithfulness, and unconditional love that feel missing sometimes from my daily routine and relationships. Those significant songs are in my heart, and my heart sings along (even if I'm not really a good singer). I often listen to songs like these when I'm walking, and, as I move along to the music, I can feel it in my lungs and bones.

Think of a song that you turn to for comfort.

- What kind of feelings does it evoke?
- What powerful words or images make it special for you?
- What memories does it stir up for you?
- Perhaps there is a ritual or routine other than listening to familiar songs that comforts you when you're feeling lonely and overwhelmed. If so, describe it.

Let Go?

There's a famous old joke that goes something like this: Once a man fell down a cliff. As he was falling, he managed to grab hold of a bush on the way down, and he hung on for dear life. He shouted back to the top of the cliff, "Is there anyone there?"

Eventually, after shouting for some time, he heard a voice say, "I am here."

"Thank goodness," said the man, "Who are you?"

"I'm God," said God.

The man was impressed and comforted. "Can you help me God?" said the man.

"Yes," God told him.

The man asked, "What do I have to do?"

God said, "Let go."

There was a pause, and then the man said, "Is there anybody else up there?"

Trusting God is no easy thing. Sometimes God calls us to things that are neither comfortable nor free of risk. In the end, we have to take God at God's word and trust. Sometimes, it is all about letting go.

- What are some of the things that you are hanging onto that if you were to let them go you would be better able to experience God's presence and love?

The Horse and His Boy

In C. S. Lewis's novel, *The Horse and His Boy*, part of the Chronicles of Narnia, the hero, Shasta, and his horse Bree are on a desperate journey to save themselves and the land of Narnia. They are stalked and pursued by lions throughout the journey. Shasta meets Aslan the lion, the Lord and protector of Narnia, toward the end of the journey. He discovers from Aslan that during all of the times he thought that he and Bree were close to death, it was, in fact, Aslan himself who was close to them, protecting them and helping them on to the next part of the journey. It turns out that the times Shasta felt most alone and frightened, he was, in fact, most closely protected by Aslan.

- Can you think of times in your life when God didn't seem to be present in the moment but, on looking back on that moment now, you can see God's closeness and protection? What might that mean for you right at this moment? Are there ways at the moment that God is close to you that you might not yet be aware of?

Mask

The film *Mask* tells the true story of Rocky Dennis, a teenage boy with a crippling bone disease. Rocky's facial bones continue to build calcium, making his face distort and take on the look of a mask. Rocky had to endure years of being shunned and stared at, yet he never seemed to let the way strangers and classmates in school saw him dictate how he saw himself. Much of the reason Rocky could see himself as truly human and as an ordinary teenage boy was because of his "family." Rocky lived with his mother and a group of bikers (themselves, pretty much rejects from "normal" society). To Rocky's mother and the biker group, Rocky was a smart, normal kid who was full of life and needed no special treatment. Rocky saw himself for who he was—loved and lovable. It didn't hurt, of course, to arrive at a new school on the back of a Harley with a huge biker named Bulldozer walking Rocky to the door and silencing the wisecracking bullies with one menacing look!

Think about what makes our self-identity. If we are constantly told from a young age that we are stupid, then, before too long, we begin to believe it. We begin to feel stupid. We feel there is no point in trying to do well in school, for instance, because we "know" we are stupid. Because we do not try, our results are poor, "proving" that we are stupid. It all becomes a vicious cycle. What if the reverse was true? What if we are constantly told that we are loved and respected, known and chosen? How might your life change if you were fully to understand and experience the love God has for you?

PRAYER
Creator God, you know me because you made me. You are the beginning and the end of all that is. I know you will never leave me alone. Amen.

THE STORY

As you read the story, look for key aspects of its descriptions of God's qualities and the nature of the beloved community.

> ¹But now thus says the Lord, he who created you, O Jacob, he who formed you, O Israel: Do not fear, for I have redeemed you; I have called you by name, you are mine. ²When you pass through the waters, I will be with you; and through the rivers, they shall not overwhelm you; when you walk through fire you shall not be burned, and the flame shall not consume you. ³For I am the Lord your God, the Holy One of Israel, your Savior. I give Egypt as your ransom, Ethiopia and Seba in exchange for you. ⁴Because you are precious in my sight, and honored, and I love

> you, I give people in return for you, nations in exchange for your life. [5]Do not fear, for I am with you; I will bring your offspring from the east, and from the west I will gather you; [6]I will say to the north, "Give them up," and to the south, "Do not withhold; bring my sons from far away and my daughters from the end of the earth— [7]everyone who is called by my name, whom I created for my glory, whom I formed and made." [8]Bring forth the people who are blind, yet have eyes, who are deaf, yet have ears! [9]Let all the nations gather together, and let the peoples assemble. Who among them declared this, and foretold to us the former things? Let them bring their witnesses to justify them, and let them hear and say, "It is true." [10]You are my witnesses, says the Lord, and my servant whom I have chosen, so that you may know and believe me and understand that I am he. Before me no god was formed, nor shall there be any after me. [11]I, I am the Lord, and besides me there is no savior. [12]I declared and saved and proclaimed, when there was no strange god among you; and you are my witnesses, says the Lord. [13]I am God, and also henceforth I am He; there is no one who can deliver from my hand; I work and who can hinder it?

YOU PUSH THE STORY

Here's your chance to take the story and push it in directions that help you discover more about it.

PUSH POSSIBILITIES FOR ISAIAH 43:1–13

- With which images of God and the beloved community did you resonate?
- Which images perturbed you or left you cold?
- Which ones were most plausible and which were least believable?
- How do you typically respond to promises others make to you?
- What's your track record for keeping promises?

THE STORY PUSHES YOU

Here's where the story pushes to you a new place of wholeness, healing, and perspective.

PUSH POSSIBILITIES FOR ISAIAH 43:1–13

- What is the meaning of your name? Is it one that you have chosen or is it one that was given to you?
- What does it mean to you to be a creature or created being of God?

- What fears about life do you have that would be comforted by words such as these of the prophet?
- How would someone who does not acknowledge the existence of God interpret or deal with this passage?

> ### THE STORY BEHIND THE STORY
> This message from the anonymous prophet Second Isaiah was a prophetic message of salvation to the community of Israel at the end of the Babylonian exile. It was apparently in the form of a liturgical exchange, communicated by a priest in response to the prayers of individuals or people. This would be closest to the confession followed by the words of absolution or reassurance in Christian worship. The oracle begins with "thus says the Lord," which is messenger language also found in the prophetic tradition including Amos, Hosea, Nehemiah, Jeremiah, and others between the eighth century and sixth century B.C.E.
>
> The words of assurance are addressed to the whole people of Israel, and the expressions "he who created you" and "he who formed you" define both the speaker and the addressee, that is, God and the people of God. The expression "do not fear" would indicate that the hearers are fearful and have expressed their fear, often in the language of prayer.
>
> The reasons given not to fear include connections to the creation of the people by God, redemption of the people from Egypt, and the intimate connection between God and God's people. "You are my witnesses and my servant whom I have chosen" shows Israel to be a single community, and single entity as God's servant. "I have called you by name, and you are mine" may be read both individually and corporately, but also refers to Israel as the beloved. God will negotiate the terms of the freeing of the people for ransom so that they can return to the land—God breaks into and controls all history.
>
> Faith assures us of God's presence not only in creation but also in our particular moments of pain, distress, and loneliness. Throughout Isaiah 40–55, the prophet proclaims that the exile is over and God will lead the people home.

PUSH OUT

- What individuals or groups in your community need to hear a message of love and solidarity? What forces are preventing them from "coming home" to comfort and freedom? Try writing a message of solidarity to one of these groups. Even if it feels beyond your capacity to deliver, what assurances and promises would you want to make? Are there ways in which you can realize some measure of the promises and hopes you have for this "beloved community"?
- Engage in random acts of kindness. Make some handmade greeting cards and hand deliver them to key people in your life telling them a little of what they mean to you. At an organization or your church, put up a handmade banner saying thanks to the group or the minister for being there.
- Think of all the commuters who travel to and from work on a road near you. Think of one wonderful thing you would like to give them, some message of hope and joy. Then write it or paint it on a huge sheet of card and take it to the side of that busy road during rush hour and hold it up. You might want to write a verse of poetry, reproduce a quote, paint a huge flower, whatever you think will lift commuters out of themselves, even if just for a moment.
- What better way to celebrate than with food? Make some chocolates and give them out in church or at school. Each time you give out a chocolate, say "Remember, God is with you."
- Get hold of some copies of daily newspapers and some wide, red marker pens. Pin or stick the sheets around the space, and invite people to take the pens and write messages of good news and hope across the stories and advertisements.
- Muslim believers are called to prayer during the day by a call from a minaret or other high point. Choose some statements from the passage (or some from other parts of the scriptures or statements you write yourself) that tell the good news of God's presence and care. "Broadcast" them from the highest point you can or through the sound system as a call to prayer prior to a service of worship.

GROUP IDEAS

Focus: To experience and live in the surprising wonder of God's love for us.

LIFE'S A PUSH
- Discuss responses to the questions on pages 64–65.
- Conclude with the prayer on page 66.

THE STORY
- With others, list the qualities of God and the beloved community that emerge from your reading of Isaiah 43:1–13.
- Choose a method for your group to experience Isaiah 43:1–13 from the selections on page 24.

YOU PUSH THE STORY
- Consider the possibilities to push this story on page 67 and invite participants to come up with their own story pushes.
- As questions arise, find suggested responses in "The Story behind the Story." How can the group find answers to questions that aren't covered in that section? Biblical reference materials, on-line commentaries, and local scholars might be good sources for further information.

THE STORY PUSHES YOU
- Imagine with the group that the passage from Isaiah is a love song from God to the people. How does it challenge or confirm members' understanding of relationship with God? with others?

PUSH OUT
Explore the "Push Out" ideas and choose one that you might pursue as a group.

6. [SHAPED BY GOD

Just like the clay in the potter's hand, so are you in my hand. . .

Jeremiah 18:6b

> Jeremiah, one of the great prophets of Israel, describes God as a potter. How is God shaping you?

LIFE'S A PUSH

The woman leaves her clay-lined basket of berries beside the hot fire as she heads off to the river to fish for the day's meal. A hungry flame licks the edge of the dry basket and it catches fire, burning away the fibers that knit it together. When the woman returns carrying the day's catch, all that is left of her former basket is a white-hot clay bowl, hardened like stone. This woman, the first potter, will gather more of the river clay and sculpt it into plump jars and slender jugs. In the lonely evenings when the moon casts a white light across her work, she will make drinking cups stained blood red with berry juice to dip into the cold river water. With a sharp stone pressed into the soft clay, she will draw the story of her life in a world before words.

My friend Jackie could be a spiritual descendent of that first potter. Her studio is a small cedar cabin set in the shade of pine and aspen trees. Friends come from all over northern Alberta, Canada, to see her latest creations. On any given visit, they might find finely sculpted pottery wolves, grouse, horses, or polar bears that have emerged from her giant white kiln. Jackie shapes beautiful sculptures that artfully describe the natural world as she experiences it. But her work is also quite practical. Her studio is full of sturdy wooden shelves that are loaded down with rusty brown pottery mugs and bowls, rough green casserole dishes, and glazed plates all fit for everyday use.

Before a potter tests his or her clay against the heat of a fire or the 700–900 degree temperatures inside a kiln, each piece must be as close to perfect as it can be. The clay has been molded and shaped until no air pockets remain within it. If objects are placed into the heat before they are ready, they explode into fragments, destroying or disfiguring whatever is in their path. Since that first clay bowl was accidentally fired, potters have learned from experience that shaping clay is a sacred trust. What is created must not only be beautiful and useful, it must also be able to withstand extremes of temperature and even the volatility of the other objects around it in the kiln.

In Jeremiah 18:1–11, the ancient prophet describes God as a potter and humanity as the clay, giving us an opportunity to explore the sacred trust of our creation through this image.

- What shape has God the potter given you? How is God continuing to shape you?
- How do you shape the world around you? How do you work together with God on that?

PRAYER
Great Artist, free us to embrace the creative, molding spirit of your love. Guide our efforts to shape a world that more resembles your image of creation. Amen.

Read the story of God as the potter and humanity as the clay from the prophet Jeremiah. Allow hope and challenge to emerge from this wheel of creative imagery.

THE STORY

Here is the story from Jeremiah 18:1–11. Select one of the ways to experience this story found on page 24. Of course, working with clay seems like a natural experience to couple with this text.

> ¹The word that came to Jeremiah from the Lord: ²"Come, go down to the potter's house, and there I will let you hear my words." ³So I went down to the potter's house, and there he was working at his wheel. ⁴The vessel he was making of clay was spoiled in the potter's hand, and he reworked it into another vessel, as seemed good to him. ⁵Then the word of the Lord came to me: ⁶Can I not do with you, O house of Israel, just as the potter has done? says the Lord. Just like the clay in the potter's hand, so are you in my hand, O house of Israel. ⁷At one moment I may declare concerning a nation or a kingdom, that I will pluck up and break down and destroy it, ⁸but if that nation, concerning which I have

Shaped by God

> spoken, turns from its evil, I will change my mind about the disaster that I intended to bring on it. ⁹And at another moment I may declare concerning a nation or a kingdom that I will build and plant it, ¹⁰but if it does evil in my sight, not listening to my voice, then I will change my mind about the good that I intended to do to it. ¹¹Now, therefore, say to the people of Judah and the inhabitants of Jerusalem: Thus says the Lord: Look, I am a potter shaping evil against you and devising a plan against you. Turn now, all of you from your evil way, and amend your ways and your doings.

YOU PUSH THE STORY

Imagine a potter turning the wheel, shaping and reshaping until a finely sculpted pot emerges from the soft rust brown clay. Explore how this image of God affects you. What attracts you, creates disturbing feelings, or gives you a new perspective? What questions do you have about this passage?

PUSH POSSIBILITIES FOR JEREMIAH 18:1–11

- How does the idea of God as potter, shaping people and their lives, challenge or support the idea of free will?
- Does God act to destroy governments that are acting in evil ways?
- Would God "frame disaster" for anyone? Why or why not?
- What about innocent people in the kingdoms God wants to destroy? Would God punish them, too? Why or why not?

THE STORY PUSHES YOU

Reflect on how the story calls each of us into account, challenging us to think about our behavior and the times when we are not faithful. Consider the ways in which this story empowers and inspires us to reshape our society and world. For example, think about:

PUSH POSSIBILITIES FOR JEREMIAH 18:1–11

- What actions do you need to turn away from? What ways of yours need mending?
- Who are you in the story: Jeremiah, the potter, or the clay? Why?
- How are you shaped by others? How do you shape the lives of others?
- What would you label as the "spoilt clay" of our world today?
- How does this story offer comfort and hope?
- What other pushes does the story have for us?

THE STORY BEHIND THE STORY

Jeremiah became a prophet in 627 B.C.E. He was probably born sometime between 645 and 640 B.C.E., and lived in Jerusalem for most of his life. Three Judean kings—Josiah, Jehoiakim, and Zedekiah—consulted, criticized, and imprisoned him. Jeremiah witnessed war, survived captivity, and weathered the political intrigue that culminated in the destruction of Jerusalem in 587 B.C.E.

The Book of Jeremiah is our most reliable source for information about the prophet and his times. It explores the political and military decisions made by those who had the power of life and death over the people of Judah. Jeremiah's anguish in the face of drought and war expresses the shared emotions and concerns of Jerusalem's guild of professional prophets. However, the Book of Jeremiah cannot be read as a journalistic account of Jeremiah's life on the frontlines of wartime Judah. It was edited long after the prophet's death. It is often difficult to determine which are the actual words of the prophet among the tales of political intrigue, laments, and visions that fill this book's pages and which are actually the work of later writers who knew how the stories turned out.

In Jeremiah 18:1–11, God is compared to a potter who shapes humanity. This would have been a familiar analogy for people living in ancient Palestine. Earlier prophets, such as Isaiah, also describe God as a potter. The creation story, in which human beings are made from the clay of the earth (Genesis 2:7), also suggests a God who crafted the universe on an infinite wheel. The destruction of clay objects, as might happen in everyday life, was a vividly real symbol of utter and permanent destruction.

Potters in ancient Palestine used earthen clay mixed with grit and water. The earliest pottery vessels were shaped by hand. Clay was sometimes pressed around the inside of a basket, which was then consumed in the firing process, leaving the finished pot. Some small objects were formed by holding a lump of clay in the palm of one hand while pinching it into shape with the other.

A person entering a potter's house in Jeremiah's time would have seen a man seated on the edge of a small pit. Inside the pit was a potter's wheel made of two large, flat stones, one designed to pivot on the other. The stones were lubricated with olive oil, and as the potter turned the wheel with his feet, the heavy aroma of warm olive oil and clay would fill the air.

Shaped by God

After being shaped on the wheel, a pot would be decorated with pebbles or shells or etched with bone tools. Traditions of pot making were passed on from generation to generation. Bowls, cups, cooking pots, lamps, jars, pitchers, spindle whorls, buttons, figurines, and toys were made of pottery. Broken shards of pottery were the "poor man's paper." People wrote notes and lists on pottery fragments—many of which have been found by modern archaeologists.

Scholars are divided over the message of the story in Jeremiah 18:1–11. Some suggest that Jeremiah was saying that God, the potter, would transform the painful events of the past into new hope for Israel. The spoiled pot could be remade into a new, stronger vessel. Other scholars suggest that the passage was predicting the coming doom of the nation, as implied in verse 11. We will probably never know with certainty which interpretation reflects Jeremiah's own thoughts. The passage remains as enigmatic as a clay sculpture that each generation will reinterpret for itself.

PUSH OUT

Consider how you might use one or more of the following ideas to further explore the story of the potter and the clay. Use these activities as an opportunity to reflect on how God may be shaping you . . . and the world through you.

- Using self-hardening clay, create symbols of God's intention for humanity. In your group, share what you have made and what your symbol means for you.
- Bring original works of art, art magazines, or art books to your session to experience and discuss. Try to show different styles of expression (e.g. pottery, paintings, pen and ink drawings, music, etc.). In what ways might engaging in the process of creative expression be a spiritual discipline or practice? Does any particular expression seem more "spiritual" than the others? Why or why not? What social commentary do the pieces offer? Do any of the pieces hint at stories or images from the Bible?
- Find other images of potters in the Bible. Refer to a Bible dictionary to track these down. Compare the images. What new insights do they offer you about the nature of God and humanity?
- Watch the film *The Red Violin* (Lions Gate Films, 1999; director, François Girard). Afterwards, discuss the symbolism of the violin. Where did the violin get its special power? How does this film inform the image of God as potter?

- Invite a potter to speak to your group about the creative process that he or she goes through in creating a new work of art or an everyday object. Read the Jeremiah passage again. What new insights emerge from the passage in light of the conversation with the potter?
- Take your group to a museum or an art gallery that displays pottery from a variety of civilizations and eras. Which of them are purely artistic, and which are also functional? Why do you think that almost every culture on earth uses and makes pottery? What can the different styles you see tell you about the communities from which these pieces come? Some of the pottery on display is richly colored and decorated, some is plain and functional. If we think about God as the potter, how do all the different styles you see speak to you about the way God works?

Shaped by God

GROUP IDEAS

Focus: To reflect on the image of the potter and the clay, and to explore the new insights it provides into the nature of God and our own calling in the world.

LIFE'S A PUSH
- Invite people to name the favorite piece of pottery they own or have seen. What is it about that object that appeals to them?
- Read aloud the introduction to this chapter. Share your reaction to the stories. Discuss the ways a potter may or may not be an appropriate image of God.
- Invite a potter to talk with the group about the experience of creating pottery: the steps involved, the feelings evoked, the successes and failures encountered.
- Offer the prayer provided on page 72 or another prayer.

THE STORY
- Choose a method to experience Jeremiah 18:1–11 from those provided on page 24.
- Brainstorm images of God from the Bible. What do the images have in common?
- Talk briefly about the context of the story from information in "The Story behind the Story" on pages 74–75. If you have an illustrated Bible dictionary or other Bible study reference, share images of ancient pottery and pottery making.

YOU PUSH THE STORY
- Distribute pieces of broken pottery and thin line black markers. Invite people to write one question about Jeremiah 18:1–11 on the inside of their potsherd. Gather the shards together. Discuss each question and share possible answers.
- Consider the push possibilities on page 73. If desired, refer to background material in "The Story behind the Story" for possible answers to some of your questions.

THE STORY PUSHES YOU
- Discuss the push possibilities provided on page 73. Invite participants to raise other questions.

Push Out

- Choose one or more "Push Out" ideas to do with the group.
- Plan a future visit to a potter's studio or pottery show. Afterwards, gather for coffee and discussion about what the artist's work expresses. Use the experience as another opportunity to explore the image of God as potter.

> **PRAYER**
>
> Potter God, be with us as we go out into the world. Shape us in ways that help us, in turn, shape our community and our world. May we be formed in your love and by that love work to form the world of the prophet's vision: a world of hope, mercy, and justice. Amen.

7. [WALK THE TALK

What does the Lord require of you but to do justice,
and to love kindness, and to walk humbly with your God?
> Micah 6:8

> Confused about the practice of religion and wondering what's at the heart of faithful living? The prophet Micah strips away all the rites and rituals that mark so much of religious practice to reach a simple, but not easy, core.

LIFE'S A PUSH

Words to Change a Heart

Four men, Baptist church elders, wrapped in light cloaks, drain their bottles of Fanta in one swallow and set them on the dirt floor of the corrugated hut. They watch as I sip at mine. The orange soda douses my throat, burning from the black smoke and dust outside. The men sit on a makeshift bed with a picture of Jesus over it. I sit on the only chair in the cramped room. In Arabic and through a series of gestures, they ask if I would pray. I say a short prayer. Then one of them in English says, "Jesus wants you and your people to pray for us. Jesus wants us to pray for your change of hearts."

The four men are from a church in a garbage collecting community in Cairo, Egypt. Families in the community survive by sorting through bits of garbage for food and materials to make their homes. The men showed me around, and then sent me away with the mandate to have a change of heart. Their words have stayed with me for years.

Sometimes we wake up to the fact that something is missing from the way we live. We feel a disconnection between what we believe and what we do. A song, an image, a news report, or a trip to a new place jars us into trying to reconnect our core values and the essence of our faith to our actions and commitments.

- How would you pray for those men and their families in the garbage dump?
- Why would they pray for my change of heart? What change were they hoping for?

Prophetic Cry

Some contemporary music can act as today's prophecy in the way that it can point out gaps between what we say we believe as a society and what we actually do. The music group Rage Against the Machine speaks out against the negative effects of global capitalism in their song "Maria" from the album *The Battle of Los Angeles*:

> Maria is a young woman who works in a sweatshop.
> And now she got a quota
> tha needle and thread crucifixion
> sold and shipped across the new line of Mason Dixon
> Rippin' through denim
> Tha point an inch from her vein
> Tha foreman approach
> His steps now pound in her brain
> His presence it terrifies
> and eclipses her days
> No minutes to rest
> No moment to pray
> And with a whisper
> He whips her
> Her soul chained to his will
> "My job is to kill if you forget to take your pill"
> Her arms jerk
> Tha sisters gather round her and scream
> as if in a dream . . ."[1]

Maria could be a woman living in any number of places: El Salvador, Indonesia, Haiti, or your hometown.

- How does the song challenge you? Our culture?
- Can you think of other prophetic songs?

Silent Sermon

Perhaps you've heard the story of the people who had to quickly pass around a man lying near the entrance to the church building on Sunday morning. His head was covered with a blanket and his clothes were old and torn. The people hurried past, awkward and uncomfortable. When it was time for the service to begin, the man walked down the center aisle and up to the front to lead worship. That was sermon enough for the people that Sunday.

Walk the Talk

The challenge to live a life true to our faith comes in many forms, most often from those who come into our range of sight and hearing from the margins.

> **PRAYER**
> Holy One, make us ready to receive your word of challenge and hope so we may learn to live our lives grounded in who we are as people of faith. We want to worship you with our whole selves, our whole lives. Amen.

The prophets came to God's people from all walks of life to bring judgment, hope, warning, and vision. The prophet Micah reminds the people of their promise with God to worship God and to take care of one another.

THE STORY

Read the words of the prophet Micah (6:1–8) that follow. Then choose one or more of the ways to experience the story found on page 24. As you read, imagine the setting as a court of law with God's people as defendants and all of creation as witness and jury.

> [1] Hear what the Lord says:
>   Rise, plead your case before the mountains,
>   and let the hills hear your voice.
> [2] Hear, you mountains, the controversy of the Lord,
>   and you enduring foundations of the earth;
> for the Lord has a controversy with his people,
>   and he will contend with Israel.
>
> [3] "O my people, what have I done to you?
>   In what have I wearied you? Answer me!
> [4] For I brought you up from the land of Egypt,
>   and redeemed you from the house of slavery;
> and I sent before you Moses, Aaron, and Miriam.
> [5] O my people, remember now what King Balak of Moab devised,
>   what Balaam son of Beor answered him,
> and what happened from Shittim to Gilgal,
>   that you may know the saving acts of the Lord."
>
> [6] With what shall I come before the Lord,
>   and bow myself before God on high?

> Shall I come before him with burnt offerings,
>   with calves a year old?
> ⁷Will the Lord be pleased with thousands of rams,
>   with ten thousands of rivers of oil?
> Shall I give my firstborn for my transgression,
>   the fruit of my body for the sin of my soul?"
> ⁸He has told you, O mortal, what is good;
>   and what does the Lord require of you
> but to do justice, and to love kindness,
>   and to walk humbly with your God?

YOU PUSH THE STORY

Take this opportunity to ask questions of the story, raise doubts and frustrations, admit curiosity, and say what attracts you about particular words and phrases. Here are some suggestions to help you get started:

PUSH POSSIBILITIES FOR MICAH 6:1–8

- Who is Balak, king of Moab and Balaam? What does "Shittim to Gilgal" mean?
- Why are the people so willing to offer burnt offerings, rams, oil, and firstborn children?
- Who is speaking in this story?
- What is "justice" and "kindness" in this story, and what does it mean to "walk humbly"?
- Who is being put on trial and why?
- What other pushes do you have?

THE STORY PUSHES YOU

Allow the prophet's story to push you. How does it challenge you and help you to clarify your sense of what faithful living is truly about?

PUSH POSSIBILITIES FOR MICAH 6:1–8

- What forms of religious ritual do you think of when you read this story from Micah?
- How are we called by Micah to do something different in terms of how we worship God?

- How does the story invite us to think about mountains, hills, and creation in general?
- How do we put the words, "Do justice, love kindness, and walk humbly with God" into practice?
- How does the story suggest we look at God's anger? Is God expressing feelings of being hurt?
- What other ways might the story judge or empower us?

> **THE STORY BEHIND THE STORY**
> Micah was an eighth century prophet born into relative poverty in a village in southern Judah (the southern kingdom that remained after Israel in the north was destroyed). He spoke out against the rich of the area around Jerusalem who devoured the poor of the land. He called them and all people to remember what kind of worship God requires: devotion to God and commitment to justice for the neighbor.
>
> Earlier in the book of Micah, the prophet warns about idols (1:7), about taking over someone else's fields and oppression (2:2), about not providing for women and children (2:9), and about building the city with "blood" (3:10). He claims that the wealthy "tear the skin from off God's people" with their economic privilege.
>
> Judah was required to pay heavy taxes to its neighbor Assyria during the time of King Hezekiah, which was also in Micah's time. The tributes that were paid fell heaviest on the peasant class who worked the land.
>
> The story is a lawsuit. The people of God have violated their covenant or promise with God. God calls the hills and the mountains as witness and jury as God pleads God's case. First God asks, "What did I do to deserve this? Did I do you wrong?" in verse 3. Then God reminds the people of all the ways that God has lived up to the covenant: (a.) brought them out of Egypt; (b.) provided the inspired leadership of Moses, the prophet, Aaron, his brother and the beginning of the priestly class, and Miriam, the woman who danced at freedom from the Egyptian army; (c.) delivered them from the schemes of Balak and Balaam when the people of Moab tried to get the Israelites cursed; and (d.) brought them into the promised land at the Jordan River at Gilgal.
>
> The defendants, the people of Judah, respond by asking if they are to offer sacrifices ranging from calves to their own firstborn. The response belies the fact that God's people have lost touch with what

> God requires. They are caught up with the religious ceremony and ritual rather than the core of this relationship with God. God reminds the people again what they already have been told in the past: Sincere worship is linked with justice and kindness and "walking humbly with God."
>
> Doing justice (*mispat*) is defined throughout the Hebrew Scripture as taking care of the sojourner, the widow, and the orphan and judging the cause of the poor and the needy. Kindness (*hesed*) is a love and loyalty of the covenant lived out by having mercy on those who are vulnerable and living bound to God's mercy. "Humbly" can most accurately be defined as "carefully" or "circumspectly." It is a walk that puts God first, each step in conformity with discernment of God's will. It is living in communion with the Holy One and those deemed "lowly."

PUSH OUT

The mantra, "do justice, love kindness, walk humbly with God," is a powerful guide for faithfulness. Choose from among these suggested ways of living into this plan for right worship and righteous living.

- Try the simple exercise of literally walking humbly with God, as described by the Zen master Thich Nhat Hanh. Nhat Hanh has spent years as a teacher to Christians in the United States, inviting a way of peace through meditation that opens us to receive the Gospel of Jesus in a new way. He writes,

    Walking meditation is walking not in order to arrive, but just to walk. The purpose is to be in the present moment and, aware of our breathing and our walking, to enjoy each step. . . . When we do walking meditation outside, we walk a little slower than our normal pace, and we coordinate our breathing with our steps. For example, we may take three steps with each in-breath and three steps with each out-breath. So we can say, "In, in, in. Out, out, out." If your lungs want four steps instead of three, please give them four steps. If they want only two steps, give them two. The lengths of your in-breath and out-breath do not have to be the same. For example, you can take three steps with each inhalation and four with each exhalation. . . . Be aware of the contact between your feet and the Earth. Walk as if you are kissing the Earth with your feet. We have caused a lot of damage to the Earth. Now it is time for us to take good care of her.[2]

- Collect prophetic contemporary music. Are there songs that match the format of a lawsuit in Micah? What are the warnings that musicians are calling us to heed? What are the forms of devotion they inspire? What are the challenges they throw out to us?
- Try a simulation game that gets you to think about economic injustice in North America or to engage in a sweatshop action in your community. The Ten Days for Global Justice Campaign of churches in Canada has wonderful resources. Check out their Web site at <www.web.net/~tendays> or write to: Ten Days for Global Justice; Suite 201, 947 Queen Street East; Toronto, Ontario, M4M 1J9. Co-op America also has good information about current sweatshop actions. They are at <www.coopamerica.org> or 1612 K Street NW, #600; Washington, D.C. 20006.
- Discuss the traditions and rituals of your faith community or group. How do they serve to connect believers with justice, kindness, and walking humbly? How do they detract from what God may be requiring? How might you communicate to your community what you think is most essential for worship?
- Focus a word study on "justice" *(mispat)* in the Hebrew Scriptures. Start by finding all the references to it in the Bible by using a concordance (an index of passages for each word used in the Bible). Look first at the way the prophets use the term and then at its use in other parts of the Hebrew Scriptures. What patterns do you discover? How would you define it based on your discoveries?

GROUP IDEAS

[Focus: To experience the meaning of Micah's prophetic core definition of faithful living.

LIFE'S A PUSH
- Bring Rage against the Machine's *The Battle of Los Angeles* or another musical album that speaks prophetically to contemporary injustices and a means to play it. Create a display of various articles of clothing over a clothesline or on a table. Include a picture of a simply dressed woman.
- Ask a participant to read "Words to Change a Heart" and discuss briefly, using the questions that follow the story.
- Play or read the lyrics from "Maria" from *The Battle of Los Angeles* or other music. Discuss the song and the questions that follow "Maria."
- Tell the story "Silent Sermon."
- Offer the prayer on page 81 or a prayer by someone in the group.

THE STORY
- Read aloud the story from Micah.
- Choose a way to experience the story from page 24. Keep in mind that art and vision exercises often work well with prophetic poetry.

YOU PUSH THE STORY
- Look together at the push possibilities on page 82 and invite the sharing of others that participants may have.
- As pushes are raised, discuss possible responses, using "The Story behind the Story" as a guide.

THE STORY PUSHES YOU
- Explore the prophet imagination of Micah—his images and visions and words. Use the push possibilities on pages 82–83 as a guide.
- Make note of those pushes that are particularly important to the group for further discussion in the "Push Out."

PUSH OUT
- Have a space available for a walking meditation. Use the instructions in the "Push Out" on page 84.
- Make available a concordance to the NRSV Bible that includes Hebrew references for pushing the word "justice." Invite the group to explore some of the uses of the word "justice" in the Scriptures. (A concordance is a book or software program that allows you to look up any word in the Bible and find all of the verses in which it appears.)

- Have resources ready for other "Push Outs."
- For a closing time, say aloud each of the three requirements: Do justice; Love kindness; Walk humbly with God; offering silence between each for participants to absorb them.

---

1. Rage against the Machine (Tim Com, Zack De La Rocha, Tom Morello, and Brad Wilk), "Maria," lyrics by Zack De La Rocha, *The Battle for Los Angeles*, compact disk (New York: Sony Music Entertainment, 1999). Used by permission.
2. Thich Nhat Hanh, *Peace Is Every Step: The Path of Mindfulness in Everyday Life*, ed. Arnold Kotler (New York: Bantam, 1991), 28.

[TASTE OF MERCY

Blessed are those who hunger and thirst for righteousness, for they will be filled.
> Matthew 5:6

> Ironically, the drive for success and happiness can dull our hearts. Jesus awakens our desire to discover joy found along a different path.

LIFE'S A PUSH

A Ripe Tomato

It was one of those sluggish Monday mornings, when I would ask myself too many big questions. You know, the "What am I doing?" questions that can turn even the brightest sunshine into a haze of self-pity. I decided to drive out to visit an acquaintance, a ninety-four-year-old woman who lives by herself in a little cottage at the end of a long, dirt road. When I pulled into the drive, she was crouched in her patch of vegetables out back, a straw hat perched on her swatch of white hair and a ripe tomato balanced in her palm. She navigated the cucumber vines with her cane to greet me, and we headed inside for shelter from the scorching July heat. She lowered herself into a chair at the kitchen table and began turning the tomato in her hand as if it were a crystal watch on a rotating display. In a soft, gravelly voice she exclaimed, "It is so red! Deep red! It is perfectly beautiful, isn't it?" Tears of joy streamed down her cheeks as we simply sat together looking at the ripe tomato. My haze lifted and the questions that had been raging in my mind simmered down.

Preserving Integrity

I had a call from a TV reporter friend. Her station had just accepted the donation of a Doppler weather radar from the area's power utility. She had been asked by the station's management not to report some of the utility's questionable environmental practices. They wanted to give her money so she would keep reporting about other things. "I have a good job. It's what I love to do and I do it well. Friends tell me, 'this is the way things are.' But I can't be happy if I feel like I have lost all my integrity," she tells me.

Gratitude for My Stupid, Little Life

The main character in the movie *American Beauty* (Dreamworks, 1999; director, Sam Mendes), Lester Burnham, confesses in the opening scenes, "In a way, I'm dead already." He looks out through the window at his wife who clips roses in the front yard. She has matching garden clogs and pruning sheers and a Smith and Hawken gardening basket cradled in one arm. Lester says, "She exhausts me just watching her. She wasn't always like this. She used to be happy. We used to be happy." That night, inside their suburban house with a red door on "Red Robin Trail," the Burnhams eat supper. The fresh roses are on the table. They eat by candlelight and "elevator music." It all seems so pretty and perfect, yet they are clearly miserable.

In the closing lines of the movie, Lester says, "I can't feel anything but gratitude for every single moment of my stupid, little life. You have no idea what I'm talking about, I'm sure. But don't worry. You will someday."[1]

Making the Connection

International lawyer Dale Recinella has arranged billion-dollar corporate deals in Florida. For seven years he had "door duty" every day at noon at a soup kitchen in Tallahassee. He would chat with street people waiting to eat. One day, an elderly woman named Helen came running into the soup kitchen. Recinella said, "A man was chasing her and threatening to kill her if she didn't give him back his dollar. 'Tell him he can't hit me 'cuz it's church property!' she pleaded." Recinella tried to mediate between them, but after twenty minutes, he said that he "bought peace by giving each of them a dollar.

"That evening," Recinella continues, "I happened to be standing on the corner of Park and Monroe. In the red twilight, I spied a lonely silhouette struggling in my direction from Tennessee Street. 'Poor street person,' I thought, as the figure inched closer. I was about to turn back to my own concerns, when I detected something familiar in that shadowy figure. The red scarf. The clear plastic bag with white border. The unmatched shoes. 'My God,' I said in my thoughts, 'that's Helen.'

"My eyes froze on her as she limped by and turned up Park. No doubt she would crawl under a bush to spend the night. My mind had always dismissed the sight of a street person in seconds. It could not expel the picture of Helen. That night as I lay on my fifteen-hundred-dollar, deluxe, temperature-controlled waterbed, I couldn't sleep. A voice in my soul kept asking, 'Where's Helen sleeping tonight?' No street person had ever interfered with my sleep. But the shadowy figure with the red scarf and plastic bag had followed me home. I had made a fatal mistake. I had learned her name."[1]

- In what ways have the characters in the stories "tasted mercy"?
- How can we move from "being dead already" to gratitude, like Lester Burnham?
- Does maintaining one's "image" ever get in the way of passion and joy? If so, how?
- How do you define happiness? What stories and experiences exemplify happiness for you?

> **PRAYER**
> We hunger and thirst for connections that move us from isolated contentment to wholeness. God, open us to the hard places, the lost lives, and the messy stories—to what's authentic. Meet us in the midst of the real, that we might experience some measure of true joy. Amen.

A blessed life is built, it seems, on deep connections not only to our own desires and comforts but to lasting values, to community, and to something beyond us. Jesus calls "blessed" those who are hurting and vulnerable and those who seek a different way of responding to others, in a story from the Gospel of Matthew.

THE STORY

Read the Bible story from Matthew 5:1–11. Then choose a way or ways to live into these sayings of Jesus from the list on page 24.

> ¹When Jesus saw the crowds, he went up the mountain; and after he sat down, his disciples came to him. ²Then he began to speak, and taught them, saying:
> ³"Blessed are the poor in spirit, for theirs is the kingdom of heaven.
> ⁴"Blessed are those who mourn, for they will be comforted.
> ⁵"Blessed are the meek, for they will inherit the earth.
> ⁶"Blessed are those who hunger and thirst for righteousness, for they will be filled.
> ⁷"Blessed are the merciful, for they will receive mercy.
> ⁸"Blessed are the pure in heart, for they will see God.
> ⁹"Blessed are the peacemakers, for they will be called children of God.
> ¹⁰"Blessed are those who are persecuted for righteousness' sake, for theirs is the kingdom of heaven.
> ¹¹"Blessed are you when people revile you and persecute you and utter all kinds of evil against you falsely on my account."

YOU PUSH THE STORY

Engage the sayings above with your uncertainties and joys and questions. What is surprising? What strikes a chord of hope? What doesn't make sense? Here is a list of possible questions. Seek response to these in "The Story behind the Story" on pages 92–93 and bring some of yours as well.

PUSH POSSIBILITIES FOR MATTHEW 5:1–11

- What does "blessed" mean?
- What is significant about Jesus teaching from a mountain?
- What is the relationship between Jesus, the crowd, and the disciples?
- It almost sounds like God's people are sort of pushovers. What does "meek" mean?
- What do "poor in spirit" and "pure in heart" mean?
- Are these requirements of faith, or statements about the way things really are, or somehow both?
- What does Jesus mean by "kingdom of heaven"?
- What other pushes do you have?

THE STORY PUSHES YOU

Allow the story to engage your life and perspectives with the way it challenges, heals, offers hope, or unsettles you.

PUSH POSSIBILITIES FOR MATTHEW 5:1–11

- What does the passage suggest about happiness?
- Who receives the rewards of God in this story? Would you include yourself among those who are rewarded? Why or why not?
- What do the sayings suggest about the meaning of success in God's eyes? What do they say about those whom the world deems "unsuccessful"?
- Can we achieve God's love and mercy or does it just come to us?
- How do the sayings alert us to connections with the poor, the hurting, and the persecuted?
- If we really take these sayings seriously, what changes would we make in our lifestyle, our jobs, and our family decisions?
- How are we satisfied? How do we taste mercy? How do we see God?
- In what other ways do the sayings push you?

THE STORY BEHIND THE STORY

These sayings of Jesus are often called "the Beatitudes," from Latin for a series of declarations about people who are fortunate, privileged, or congratulated. We translate the Greek word *makarioi* as "blessed" or in a state of being well off. The form of these declarations is borrowed from the wisdom sayings of the Hebrew Scripture.

Jesus speaks to the disciples, sitting down with them on the mountain. At this point in Matthew's story, Jesus has called only four disciples. For the gospel writer, these four represent the church that later hears the whole story as Matthew writes it. These sayings are part of a larger "Sermon on the Mountain," which Jesus gives the disciples. Later, we find out that the crowds have been listening in (7:28).

With Jesus up on the mountain, we are reminded of Moses receiving the tablets of the Ten Commandments while on a mountain. In what Jesus says, we are further reminded of the prophet Isaiah who speaks to the people of Israel after they have come back from exile in Babylon. Isaiah seeks to encourage them, saying, "The Lord has anointed me; he has sent me to bring good news to the oppressed . . . to comfort all who mourn" (Isaiah 61:1–2).

One of the characteristics of the kingdom of God is that it is present with us and to us now and at the same time we wait in hope for the Kingdom to be fully revealed; what we often describe as "now and not yet." The Beatitudes work in exactly the same way. They both point to the future ("they shall be comforted") and speak of the present moment ("theirs is the kingdom of heaven"). Dietrich Bonhoeffer, the Lutheran pastor who stood up to and was executed by the Nazis, wrote, "All are called to be what in the reality of God they already are."[2] The blessings of the Beatitudes are, therefore, a wonderful promise of what we can now experience as followers of Jesus and, at the same time, a powerful prophetic claim of what God is bringing to be. We remember, too, that these Beatitudes are not a checklist for individuals but rather a call and a promise to the whole community of humanity.

This is a different message than a similar group of sayings in Luke's Gospel gives us. Luke uses "you" to address the rich and the poor with blessings and curses: "Blessed are you who are poor, for yours is the kingdom of God" and "Woe to you who are rich, for you have received your consolation" (Luke 6:20, 24).

Different from Luke's, Matthew's Gospel talks about the "poor in spirit." There is a great deal of debate about what that means. Certainly, it means those who are literally poor, hungry, thirsty, or mourning. But it also might include those who know that they are not in control of their lives. It might be about those who don't find security by what they know or have or achieve, but instead depend on God. God's people have an identity as people who renounce the violent and unjust methods of this world's powers. Because they stand against this kind of power, they suffer for it. Because they reject the world's understandings of security, success, and happiness, they hunger and thirst.

It is clear that this blessing does not just come to those who individually "have good spirits." God is biased in favor of the poor and the hungry and those who genuinely lament along with them the injustice of the world.

Jesus' disciples are to be those who literally hunger and thirst for righteousness. They are to mourn over the inequitable distribution of the things of life. They are to seek the replacement of oppression with liberation "on earth as it is in heaven."

To have faith, according to these sayings, is not a recipe for the Good Life. These are not simply "Be-happy-attitudes," as some have suggested. It is a way of living fully convinced that God's way is *the* way to peace with justice for the whole of creation. It is living the conviction that God is bringing about righteousness and mercy for those who depend on this vision. Blessedness means finding joy in the pain of accompanying one another on a journey towards eliminating violence and injustice. This story assures us that even in the pain, the suffering, and the uncertainty of such a journey, we can experience the beauty of our lives in God.

PUSH OUT

Consider some of the following ways to experience the sayings of Jesus in this story. Use them to help you define more clearly how you are blessed in standing with the poor, the mourners, the hungry, the peacemakers, and those persecuted.

- View the movie *American Beauty*. Where do you see "blessedness" in the movie? Contrast the philosophy that states, "In order to be successful, one must project an image of success at all times," with a search for a benevolent force behind the beauty of life.

- Discuss the meaning of the Beatitudes with people in different life circumstances. Interview a group of children about their understanding of these verses. Ask them to create artwork that corresponds to one of the sayings or create a collage together using magazine images, words, or drawings to reflect your discussion of the verses. You could do a similar exercise with elders in your community or with persons with developmental disabilities.
- Engage in storytelling. In community with others committed to looking at the idea of joy from a spiritual perspective, share stories of times of satisfaction and fulfillment and comfort. Celebrate together those moments and pray for a deepening sense of God's blessedness in your experiences.
- If you have engaged in community-service kinds of "Push Outs" through other sessions, such as serving meals or visiting persons in institutional settings, strive to find a situation that will put you in contact with the same person or persons over the course of months. How can you deepen those relationships and receive the full fruits of that "knowing."
- We often hear talk about "the face of poverty." Engage in a local campaign to put a realistic, human face on poverty in your community. Find out, through human service agencies in your area, what people are affected by decisions to change welfare or social service support or move jobs elsewhere. What are their stories? Submit specific stories to your local newspaper. Create a skit to tell these stories. Offer them up as mission moments in your community of faith. Set up a visual arts display in your church on the faces of those affected by local government or economic decisions.

Taste of Mercy

GROUP IDEAS

Focus: To more deeply define joy for ourselves through engagement with the Beatitudes.

LIFE'S A PUSH
- Place something beautiful in the center of the gathering space. This could be a flower, a piece of fruit, leaves, seedpods, or something you have made. Invite participants to talk about the beauty they perceive in that object.
- Read one or more of the scenarios "A Ripe Tomato," "Preserving Integrity," "Gratitude for My Stupid, Little Life," or "Making the Connection."
- Discuss the questions on page 90.
- Read the prayer on page 90 or offer one of yours.

THE STORY
- Have each participant read one saying from the list of sayings in the story from Matthew.
- Choose a Bible experience method from suggestions on page 24. Art or writing may be particularly good ways to experience this story. Working with the meaning of words also can enrich this exploration.

YOU PUSH THE STORY
- Ask the group to raise questions, concerns, or celebrations about the sayings of Jesus included in the story.
- Share something of the other content of the Sermon on the Mount from Matthew in 5:1—7:28 (Lord's Prayer, the call to love enemies, metaphors of salt and light). Talk about the impact of these teachings as a whole. What are the common threads?
- Share responses to questions using "The Story behind the Story" as a guide.

THE STORY PUSHES YOU
- Invite group members to each select one saying and offer up ways that it challenges their thinking about success.
- Look at the push possibilities on page 91.

PUSH OUT
- Prepare for one or more of the "Push Outs" listed and lead the group through the experience.
- Offer the prayer below or one of your own.

> **PRAYER**
> May we risk looking for blessing in the hard places, God, and find joy in the connections we discover there. Amen.

1. Jim Wallis, *Faith Works: Lessons from the Life of an Activist Preacher* (New York: Random House, 2000), 30.
2. Dietrich Bonhoeffer, *The Cost of Discipleship* (New York: Macmillan, 1966), 97.

9. [BLOWING THE LID OFF "FAIR"

Take what belongs to you and go; I choose to give to this last the same as I give to you.
> Matthew 20:14

> We often think in terms of entitlement: We have expectations about what we think we deserve. Jesus tells a story of giving the full wage to those who show up at the end of the day, signaling another way to think about God's generosity . . . and our own.

LIFE'S A PUSH

Much of life seems to be about earning our fair share—not only in terms of making a living, but also in terms of our relationships, our standing in the community, and our overall fulfillment. Does anyone ever do anything without expecting some kind of just reward? Does anyone do anything just because it's the right thing to do?

DEAD MAN WALKING
In the movie *Dead Man Walking* (Polygram Video, 1995; director, Tim Robbins), Sister Helen Prejean accompanies a man to his death by the death penalty. Though he is a convicted murderer, she stands by him in his quest to find some kind of peace. He seeks a sense of self-acceptance, even as he recognizes how much suffering his violent actions have caused. Would you be willing to help him find it?

RESTORATIVE JUSTICE
On the morning of June 9, 1998, in the chapel of the Hughes Correctional Facility in Texas, Ann Hines sat across the table from the murderer of her son Paul. Next to her sat a mediator, with whom she had worked intensively for over eighteen months in preparation for this moment.

Hines dabbed the tears in her eyes and sought the strength to speak. "This is so hard for me," she said to the man who murdered her son. "And I know it's hard for you. The hardest thing, though, was to bury Paul."

The inmate, a man named White, had been waiting apprehensively and listening intently. When Hines spoke, he hung his head as tears welled up in his eyes. Hines choked back her sobs. "I appreciate your doing this," she said, "and please know that I will not be unkind to you in any way. That's not why I'm here."

White lowered his head even further. "You were the last person to see Paul alive, and it's really important that I know the last things he said and the last things that happened in his life," Hines continued.

White took a few moments to reply. "I don't know how to start," he said in barely more than a whisper. "I don't know how to explain. It was just a stupid thing. Just stupid."

After eight hours of highly charged, emotional conversation like this, Ann Hines left the encounter saying, "I went in there totally for me, but it changed for me as he listened to me, and I listened to him. At one point I remember saying, 'If you knew how much I loved him you wouldn't have shot him, I just know you wouldn't' and he just folded. . . . That sad, troubled boy let me see inside his soul. I began to feel such compassion."

White and Hines were participants in a growing movement that brings perpetrators of violent crime together with the victims or their families after long periods of study and reflection. The movement, called Restorative Justice, focuses on moving people through their anger and pain to rebuilding their lives.[1]

Hugging Luna

For 738 days, forest activist Julia Butterfly Hill lived 180 feet above the ground in the canopy of an ancient redwood she named "Luna." As loggers with the Pacific Lumber-Maxxam Corporation felled giant redwoods all around her, within deadly range at times, she stayed put in Luna. Julia, with great help from steelworkers and environmentalists, successfully negotiated permanent protection for the tree and a nearly three-acre buffer zone around it. She came down to a world that recognized the value of old trees—and the environment in general—just a tiny bit more.[2]

- What do the people in these stories, and the tree, deserve?
- What is your response to the generosity of some in these stories?
- Are "being fair" and "justice" the same things in these stories? Why or why not?
- Name some examples from your experience of persons acting on conviction when almost everyone else thought it was too late to change anything.

Blowing the Lid off "Fair"

> **PRAYER**
> God, open us to your amazing possibilities for our lives, for the lives of others, and for your creation, even when we think things are hopeless. We want to experience your amazing grace, God, that renews life. May we be both recipients of and extensions of your generosity. Amen.

Jesus tells a parable in the gospel of Matthew that suggests to us a whole new understanding of justice and participation in God's community. Experience the world of this parable.

THE STORY

Read the Bible story from Matthew 20. Decide on one or more ways to experience the story from the list on page 24.

> ¹"For the kingdom of heaven is like a landowner who went out early in the morning to hire laborers for his vineyard. ²After agreeing with the laborers for the usual daily wage, he sent them into his vineyard. ³When he went out about nine o'clock, he saw others standing idle in the marketplace; ⁴and he said to them, 'You also go into the vineyard, and I will pay you whatever is right.' So they went. ⁵When he went out again about noon and about three o'clock, he did the same. ⁶And about five o'clock, he went out and found others standing around; and he said to them, 'Why are you standing here idle all day?' ⁷They said to him, 'Because no one has hired us.' He said to them, 'You also go into the vineyard.' ⁸When evening came, the owner of the vineyard said to his manager, 'Call the laborers and give them their pay, beginning with the last and then going to the first.' ⁹When those hired about five o'clock came, each of them received the usual daily wage. ¹⁰Now when the first came, they thought they would receive more; but each of them also received the usual daily wage. ¹¹And when they received it, they grumbled against the landowner, ¹²saying, 'These last worked only one hour, and you have made them equal to us who have borne the burden of the day and the scorching heat.' ¹³But he replied to one of them, 'Friend, I am doing you no wrong; did you not agree with me for the usual daily wage? ¹⁴Take what belongs to you and go; I choose to give to this last the same as I give to you. ¹⁵Am I not allowed to do what I choose with what belongs to me? Or are you envious because I am generous?' ¹⁶So the last will be first, and the first will be last."

YOU PUSH THE STORY

Push the story from Matthew with your frustrations, questions, uncertainties, and hopes. What would you want to say to Jesus after hearing his parable? Here are some suggestions to get you started. Find some responses to them in the "Story behind the Story" on pages 101–02.

PUSH POSSIBILITIES FOR MATTHEW 20:1–16

- How do you respond to this story? Do you resonate with the ones in the story who find the landowner unfair?
- How are wages connected to the realm of God?
- Is the landowner supposed to be God?
- Where else in his teachings does Jesus use the concept "the first shall be last"? Why is this a common theme in his ministry?
- How else would you like to push the story?

THE STORY PUSHES YOU

In spite of the frustration this story from Jesus may create in terms of our usual way of thinking about what is fair, it is meant to open up our perspective. Consider ways that it may do that in our contemporary lives.

PUSH POSSIBILITIES FOR MATTHEW 20:1–16

- How does the story function to surprise us or turn our expectations upside down?
- How does the story challenge us with the meaning of "first" and "last"?
- What might this story be saying about God's acceptance and love?
- Does this story have anything to say to faith communities about membership and who's in and who's out?
- What does this say about God's measure of people?
- How might the story judge our grumbling, jealousy, or resentment of the good fortune of others?
- In what other ways does the story heal, challenge, give hope, judge, or empower you?

THE STORY BEHIND THE STORY

Jesus tells a parable in this story. A parable is a short story that uses the circumstances of everyday living to illustrate the ways of God. *Parabole*, in Greek, means literally "to throw beside." So Jesus throws an example from common knowledge next to its parallel in the reign of God. These comparisons hook the hearers through the familiar and then shock them with the way things turn out. The stories turn things upside down and, in doing so, provide a glimpse into how God operates against our expectations of the way things are. Parables are like nuts: Listeners have to crack them open to get at the meat of the matter.

In trying to crack open a parable, it is a good idea to look for the place in the story where our expectations most clash with the way God chooses to operate. In this story, verse 15 is the climax of the tension. The landowner says, "Am I not allowed to do what I chose with what belongs to me? Or are you envious that I am generous?" Listeners could rightfully expect the workers to be paid according to a normal wage structure based on time worked. But that isn't what happens.

Jesus strings the hearer along by describing first how the workers who show up late get paid exactly what the landowner says he would pay those who showed up early in the morning. Everyone would be expecting the early morning workers to be paid more than expected. But they also are paid only what the landowner promised. Now things are completely out of kilter.

Jesus is suggesting a different understanding of justice and the notion of what's right. In fact, in the world of the story, value or worth is determined not by what is right but by acceptance. It's not wages or hierarchy that count but the call to go into the vineyard with God.[3]

We cannot assume that the landowner is God. Nor can we assume that the laborers match up to particular kinds of people entering God's reign. We only know that the action and response of the landowner is what Jesus wants us to remember as the way the reign of God functions. God gives lavishly to all who need. We as human beings can object to that lavishness—to its fairness or the way it flies in the face of traditional business values. But just as the landowner has a preference for those "whom no one has hired," God has a preference for those in need.

The story is not an example of how to run a business. It's a picture of how God offers mercy and acceptance—this mysterious system often called grace.

> In the narrative just prior to this story, Jesus is interacting with someone who asks what one must do to have eternal life. Jesus says, "Go, sell all your possessions and give your money to the poor." The person who asked goes away grieving, being one with many possessions. Then Jesus says, "It is easier for a camel to go through the eye of the needle than for someone who is rich to enter the kingdom of God."
>
> We really are all workers who show up at the end of the day and need a day's wage. Nothing we do can ever earn what God gives. God simply gives out of God's abundance.

PUSH OUT

May these suggested "Push Outs" help you glimpse God's reign of generosity and acceptance.

- Watch the movie *Dead Man Walking* and discuss the accompaniment Sister Prejean provides to the death row inmate. Explore the implications of this parable for arguments in support of and in opposition to the death penalty. Consider engaging in education and action about the death penalty. If available, listen to the movie's sound track, a diverse collection of spirit-filled songs. To enhance the discussion, bring in information from Murder Victims' Families for Reconciliation, Inc. Their Web address is <www.mvfr.org>.
- Learn more about the restorative justice movement. Find out if there are opportunities for mediation between victims and offenders in your area. Consider inviting a mediator to talk with your group about this work. Resources are available through the Center for Restorative Justice and Mediation, 386 McNeal Hall, 1985 Buford Avenue, St. Paul, Minnesota 55108 or the Mennonite Central Committee on Crime and Justice, 2501 Allentown Road, Quakertown, Pennsylvania 18951.
- Consider taking a stand in your community to preserve a tree, a stretch of green space, a native rare species, a wetland, or some other local environmental gem.
- Read some of the other parables in Matthew. How do the stories in this gospel compare to their parallel versions in the other gospels? Use a gospel-parallel resource book or a concordance to locate several parables in each of the gospels. Reading them out loud or circling different words and phrases can help you discover nuances. How do you interpret these differences? What do you discover about parables and their role in the faith community past and present?

- List ways that we try to earn the gifts of God or measure the gifts that we receive. Offer them up as a prayer of confession to God, asking for a renewed sense of gratitude and openness to the generosity that is so much at the heart of God's realm that is both now and not yet. How might you ask to have your own generosity expanded?

GROUP IDEAS

Focus: To encounter God's generosity as free and independent of our good works.

Life's a Push
- In the center of the gathering area, place some time cards, pay stubs, a watch, or other measure of time worked. Ask group members to share their responses to the items: What feelings and experiences come to mind?
- Select one or more vignettes on pages 97–98 and read them aloud.
- Discuss the questions included in "Life's a Push" on page 98.
- Offer the prayer included or one of yours.

The Story
- Read the story aloud from Matthew 20.
- Select a method of experiencing the story from suggestions on page 24. Acting out parables is often illuminating, as is taking a close look at the repetition and structure of the story.

You Push the Story
- Ask participants for ways they would like to push the story with questions or reactions.
- List pushes on newsprint for further discussion.
- Add relevant pushes from the list of possibilities on page 100.
- Use "The Story behind the Story" to explore the questions that are raised. How will you find answers to questions not covered in that section? Consider asking for volunteers to find out more from biblical commentaries to bring back to the group at a later date.

The Story Pushes You
- Invite participants to spend five minutes alone with the story, asking them to explore in silence the ways it offers healing, judgment, or fresh insight.
- Come back together as a group and discuss these discoveries.
- Include in the discussion relevant push possibilities included on page 100.

Push Out
- Prepare for one or more of the "Push Out" ideas by having resources ready.
- Engage in or plan for one or more of the "Push Outs."
- Close with a prayer of yours or the one below.

> **PRAYER**
> God, you surprise us, even frustrate us with your radical generosity. Give us the courage to respond with gratitude and generosity of our own. Amen.

1. Jon Wilson, "Crying for Justice," *Hope Magazine* no. 21, (winter 2000): 52–57. Web site: <www.hopemag.com>.
2. Circle of Life Foundation Web site <www.circleoflifefoundation.org>.
3. Bernard Brandon Scott, *Hear Then the Parable: A Commentary on the Parables of Jesus* (Minneapolis: Fortress Press, 1989), 297.

10. [WHO GETS WHAT?

"Give therefore to the emperor the things that are the emperor's and to God the things that are God's."
Matthew 22:21

Many of us have a good idea of what belongs to the "emperor." But what exactly belongs to God?

LIFE'S A PUSH

The only things we can count on in life are death and taxes.
—Popular saying

I leave it to the last minute every year. The tax form in its clean manila envelope sits unopened on my desk, reminding me that I will pay dearly for my procrastination. A few days before the final filing date, I madly scramble to find bank statements and receipts, sharpen my pencils and grab my calculator. How much will I have to give to the emperor this time?

For many Christians, taxes are not simply a matter of filing dates and write-offs. They are reflections of their faith. A photograph of two American tax resisters graces the cover of an issue of *Sojourners*, a Christian social justice magazine. The young couple in the photograph is withholding their taxes to protest the use of government funds for weapons production. In another Christian publication, *The United Church Observer*, a pastor calls for the Canadian government to stop cutting taxes and start directing more money to helping the poor.

In Matthew 22:15–22, Jesus says that we should give to the emperor what is the emperor's and give to God what is God's. The Christian activists in *Sojourners* and the *Observer* are being very intentional about what they give to the emperors of our time. Their decisions are based on what they believe should be given to God: peace and an end to poverty.

- What do you think God requires of you?
- Who are the "emperors" in your life?

Whose Money is It Anyway?

Clive lives on the streets. He never has more than a few cents in his pocket at any one time. A couple of years ago, Clive found fifty dollars, a lot of money for a guy on the streets. He took it to a worker he trusted in the shelter that he often stopped into for a meal and the occasional shower. Clive wanted to know if he should hand the money in to someone somewhere. The worker told him that no one would ever be able to figure out where it came from and that he should keep it. The worker asked Clive what he might do with the money, whether he wanted the shelter to hold it for him so he could spend a little at a time, as he needed to. Clive thought for a moment, smiled, said "no, thank you" and left. The next day, by talking to some of the other men who used the shelter, the worker discovered that, the evening before, Clive had taken his precious fifty dollars, bought beer and wine, and treated all of his friends to a big party.

Neil is not a criminal. That needs to be made quite clear up front. Neil has never intentionally broken any laws. Never murdered anyone, never broken into a bank, never even taken the odd pen or box of paper clips from work. Sure, he's collected his fair share of parking tickets and speeding tickets, but nothing more than that. Neil is no criminal. Being "creative" in filing a tax return, being "economical" with the truth or staying silent on one or two issues, that's not stealing is it? It's not breaking any laws, Neil is certain of that. He pays his accountant good money to find legal ways to minimize his tax, and what's wrong with that?

Money Isn't Everything

John was nineteen when his name came up in a lottery that the government in Australia had instituted to choose who amongst the country's young men would be required to serve in the armed forces in the Vietnam conflict. Up until that very day, John had given little thought to what he believed about almost everything. He was a Christian but more because he had be brought up in a Christian home than from personal conviction. Now, however, he was confronted with a real and life-changing choice: to turn up at the recruiting office, as the official letter he had received required, or do as some other young men were doing as a witness to their faith and refuse to cooperate with the government. John knew the likely outcome of any refusal to comply with his conscription notice; the papers were full of the stories.

John had four choices. He could comply, be conscripted, be trained, be sent to Vietnam, and, most likely, be required to attempt to kill other human beings. He could ignore the order, as others were doing, go on the run, and attempt to avoid capture until the conflict was over. He could attempt to lie and persuade the courts that he was and had always been a convinced committed pacifist. Finally, he could publicly defy the order and face arrest and a prison term. After much thought and prayer, John decided that he could not be a follower of Jesus and agree to be involved in the Vietnam conflict. He also decided that he needed to own this decision and its consequence. So, on the day that he was required to, he attend the conscription office with the support of his parents and a couple of friends, informed the officer in charge that he had no intention of complying with the conscription order, was arrested, sentenced, convicted and sent to prison. Some moments in life present you with stark choices. You either follow what you know in your heart to be right or you risk losing all contact with your true self. Sometimes you really do have to choose.

- As this story suggests, money may not be the only thing we are required to "render." What else might you be required to give to "emperors"? to God?
- What is your reaction to John's decision? What would you have done and why?

> **PRAYER**
>
> Loving God, at times the world seems so complicated. We don't always know how to make the choices that are required of us. Help us discern what we need to do in order to be faithful to you. Amen.

THE STORY

Jesus was often challenged to answer complex, nearly impossible questions. Read the story in Matthew 22:15–22 to find out how Jesus responded to a question about taxes, loyalty, and faith.

> [15]Then the Pharisees went and plotted to entrap him in what he said. [16]So they sent their disciples to him, along with the Herodians, saying, "Teacher, we know that you are sincere, and teach the way of God in accordance with truth, and show deference to no one; for you do not regard people with partiality. [17]Tell us, then, what you think. Is it lawful to pay taxes to the emperor, or not?" [18]But Jesus, aware of their malice, said, "Why are you putting me to the test, you hypocrites? [19]Show me the coin used for the tax." And they brought him a denarius. [20]Then he said to them, "Whose head is this, and whose title?" [21]They answered, "The emperor's." Then he said to them. "Give therefore to the emperor the things that are the emperor's and to God the things that are God's." [22]When they heard this, they were amazed; and they left him and went away.

Who Gets What?

YOU PUSH THE STORY

Explore the characters, questions, and answers in this story from the Gospel of Matthew. Notice the interplay between Jesus and the religious leaders. What is the context of this story? What was happening around Jesus at the time? in the community for whom this gospel was first recorded? Look at "The Story behind the Story" for some further information to help you answer your own questions and respond to the push possibilities listed below.

Push Possibilities for Matthew 22:15–22

You may wish to use some of the following push possibilities to get you started:

- What was "Herod's party"?
- Who were the Pharisees? Why were they trying to "trap" Jesus?
- Do you believe the Pharisees were being genuine when they said that Jesus was a sincere teacher? Why would they have made this remark?
- Who was the emperor? What were the consequences of not paying taxes to him?
- What coin was used to pay the tax? Why didn't Jesus have a coin of his own? What seems to be significant about this detail?
- Does God want money? Why or why not?

THE STORY PUSHES YOU

Allow the story in Matthew 22:15–22 to push you. Does it pose any challenges to the way you live your life today? Does it confirm some of your convictions? How might it give you new insights into the realities of economic injustice in our times?

Push Possibilities for Matthew 22:15–22

- How would you have answered the Pharisee's question?
- What are the connections between how we spend money each day and our faith?
- Have you ever been faced with a question that didn't seem to have just one right, ethically sound answer? If so, what was the question and how did you answer it?
- How and what do you give to God?
- What do you give to the emperor? Can giving to God and giving to the emperor ever be the same? If yes, when and how?

THE STORY BEHIND THE STORY

In Jesus' time, taxes were the oil that kept the machinery of the Roman state going. Large taxes were levied on land and certain goods, including slaves. The tax on land may have equaled one-quarter or one-fifth of the produce of the land. Tax collectors (also known as publicans) went from town to town annually to collect this money. Many used their role as publican to extort additional monies from villagers for themselves.

Temple taxes were also levied against all Jews. These were paid on the basis of one-tenth share of the harvest, or a "tithe." Farmers also had to give the "first fruits" of harvest and the "firstborn" of livestock to the temple in Jerusalem as sacrificial offerings. Most people lived in the countryside and eked out a living from the land and paid their taxes accordingly. For city dwellers, taxes were based on property ownership. The people of Jerusalem paid what was known as a "house tax."

Whether they lived in city, village, or countryside, all adult males were charged an annual temple tax of one denarius. A likeness of the Roman emperor appeared on one side of this large silver coin. The reverse side was inscribed with the words "Tiberius Caesar, Son of the Divine Augustus, Pontifex Maximus."

In Matthew 22:15–22, Jesus is confronted by a group of Herodians and Pharisees. Herodians were probably a political party that supported the right of Herod the Great's successors to rule Palestine. The Pharisees were Jewish religious leaders who believed, among other things, that Jews should obey their Roman rulers as long as this did not conflict with their religious beliefs and practices.

The question that the Pharisees and Herodians put to Jesus is complex. If Jesus argues against paying taxes to the emperor, then his enemies could justifiably accuse him of sedition against Rome. If Jesus supports the tax, then the peasants and laborers who make up his followers could turn against him. Rebellion against taxation was infrequent, but not unheard of.

In answer to the Pharisees, Jesus asks to see a denarius. The denarius was the usual salary paid to a laborer for one day's work. That Jesus did not have this coin may indicate that he was extremely poor.

Most of the original hearers of the Gospel of Matthew would have understood this story to indicate that Jesus believed it was acceptable to pay taxes to the emperor. This gospel was written by and for the young churches of the Mediterranean. Its members were Jews and Gentiles

Who Gets What? 111

> who may have had little sympathy for Jewish resistance movements in Palestine. They wanted to blend in with the cultures in which they lived, steering a politically safe course while still maintaining their distinctive religion.

PUSH OUT

Find ways to explore the connections between this story and your everyday life. Also reflect on what this story might have to say about today's political, social, and economic realities. Here are some ideas to help you get started.

- Brainstorm a list of the emperors of our world. If you're working in a group, record the list on flip paper and talk about giving to them. When, if ever, is it appropriate to not give to them? Are there constructive ways to resist their rule? Are there good reasons to?
- What does it mean to "give to God, what is God's"?
- Search the Internet for charts and statistics showing how wealth is divided in the United States. How do you interpret it in terms of what is being given to God and what is being given to the emperor? What can you do to challenge this distribution, if you believe it's unbalanced? You may want to participate in the actions around globalization and debt undertaken by such Christian groups as:

Ten Days for Global Justice
Suite 201
947 Queen St East
Toronto, Ontario
Canada M4M 1J9
Phone: 877.403.8933
This ecumenical organization promotes education and advocacy about a variety of issues related to developing countries.

Bread for the World
Suite 500
50 F Street NW
Washington DC 20001
Phone: 202.639.9400/800.82.BREAD
Fax: 202.639.9401
Web site: <www.bread.org>
According to their Web site, "Bread for the World is a nationwide Christian citizens movement seeking justice for the world's hungry people by lobbying our nation's decision makers."

GROUP IDEAS

[Focus: To explore Jesus' answer to a tough question—"give therefore to the emperor the things that are the emperor's and to God the things that are God's"—and the challenges it may pose to the ways we live.

LIFE'S A PUSH
- Read aloud the opening story about taxes. Invite people to share what they think about taxes. After a brief discussion, ask them to compare taxes with offerings.
- Discuss the famous quote about death and taxes. What are people's reactions to it?
- Say the prayer provided or one of yours.

THE STORY
- Use one of the methods for your group to read Matthew 22:15–22 provided on page 24. Alternatively, give everyone a coin to hold and focus on as one person reads the story aloud, stopping just after the Pharisees ask "are we or are we not permitted to pay taxes to the Roman emperor?" Ask people to look at their coins and talk briefly in pairs about what answer they might have given to the question. Then gather in the large group and have the volunteer read the rest of the story. Invite the group to discuss any new insights or questions that emerged for them during this reading and discussion.

YOU PUSH THE STORY
- Gather any questions group members have about the story and record them on a flip chart.
- Explore these questions together with the push possibilities for Matthew 22:15–22, using the information provided in "The Story behind the Story" or a Bible dictionary to spark new insights into the text.

THE STORY PUSHES YOU
- Discuss what makes group members uncomfortable about this story. How does it push people to rethink their values or actions?
- Consider the questions provided on page 109. Also discuss other pushes that arise from the group. Does the story push the group to think or act differently together?

PUSH OUT
- Look at the "Push Out" suggestions and choose one or two that might be of interest to your group.
- Close with prayer.

11. [BEARERS OF JUSTICE

Here am I, the servant of the Lord; let it be with me according to your word.
> Luke 1:38

> So often we set goals for ourselves in competition with others and up against our own expectations of what we should achieve. Mary's openness to God's call shifts our perspective to a much more radical sense of purpose.

LIFE'S A PUSH

Most of us experience some amount of challenge just getting through the day, week, or month. Imagine on top of all the little decisions of everyday having to make one single decision that would change your life forever. In the first half of the last century, young adults in North America had to decide how they would participate in or support efforts in two world wars. Then, another generation of young adults chose their roles in the Korean and Vietnam conflicts, including resistance and protest. Those moments of decision in the face of major events probably seem clearer and more life-determining than the host of smaller decisions that we face today as we put together lives of meaning and purpose. A sense of calling in times of peace and prosperity might be seen as growing out of a collection of decisions, both for and against opportunities and directions, that accumulate into a path.

- How are you working on your sense of calling? Was there a moment in which you made the one single determining vocational decision or are you following a path of small decisions that will eventually form an overall direction?

THE ROAD NOT TAKEN

> Two roads diverged in a yellow wood,
> And sorry I could not travel both
> And be one traveler, long I stood
> And looked down one as far as I could
> To where it bent in the undergrowth;
> Then took the other, as just as fair,
> And having perhaps the better claim,
> Because it was grassy and wanted wear;
> Though as for that the passing there
> Had worn them really about the same,
> And both that morning equally lay
> In leaves no step had trodden black.
> Oh, I kept the first for another day!
> Yet knowing how way leads on to way,
> I doubted if I should ever come back.
> I shall be telling this with a sigh
> Somewhere ages and ages hence:
> Two roads diverged in a wood, and I
> I took the one less traveled by,
> And that has made all the difference.
>   —Robert Frost (1936)[1]

This is probably Frost's most famous poem, known and loved by millions of people around the world.

- How often do you think we are presented in life with two roads, two ways of going forward?
- Can you think of moments in your own life when you have had the courage to take the "road less traveled by?"

THE KIDS IN THE CHARIOT

How do you know the moment in which you live? Who is able to grasp the significance of their time? Was there anyone who was able to predict the fall of the Berlin Wall and the end of communism?

There is an old cartoon that shows Jesus carrying the cross up the road to Golgotha. As he passes a house, we see in the window above two obviously wealthy men at a table sharing a glass of wine. Oblivious of the scene being enacted below, one says to the other, "Yeah, I thought I'd chuck the kids in the chariot and head down to the coast for the weekend."

- Think about what is happening globally right now; think about your local community, and think about what is happening among those with whom you live. Imagine looking back on this moment from a decade on. What would you say was really going on at this time? What do you think is the significance of this global, community, family moment?

AIDS

During the 1980s, when AIDS was becoming a frightening reality across the world and there was fear everywhere that the virus could be caught from breath, touch, and even toilet seats, a young high-school student contracted the virus from a blood transfusion. When it became known that the young man had AIDS, he was ostracized at his school. Many parents and students, frightened that they, too, might catch the virus, wanted this boy expelled. While the school and government authorities, never having faced an issue like this before, tried to decide what to do, the young man was forced to sit by himself in the classroom surrounded by empty desks. That is, until one young student, who watched his frightened classmate being humiliated, got up from where he sat, gathered his books, and without ceremony quietly went and sat right next to the young man. For the rest of that day, the two young men sat alone. Then, first thing the next morning, there were two more students sitting in the previously empty desks. By mid-morning the tide had turned, and, for many, the spell was broken. People saw before them not a problem or a disease, but a young man, frightened like they were. Before the end of the day, most of the desks around the young man were filled with young men and women supporting their fellow student.

- What might it take to be that one student, do you think, who looks beyond the fear to see what is truly important?
- Are there situations in your community, at the moment, to which you need to open your eyes? If you do, will you be required to make some kind of decision?

PRAYER
Gracious God, help me to be attentive to the ways in which you are calling me. Give me the courage to make decisions that lead me down a path of true purpose. Help me to imagine and respond to the vision you have for my life. Amen.

Bearers of Justice

THE STORY

Read Luke 1:26–56 , which follows. You might consider reading it with four different voices: Mary, Gabriel, Elizabeth, and a narrator. How does this help you experience the drama of this story? Then select one of the methods of experiencing the story on page 24.

> [26]In the sixth month the angel Gabriel was sent by God to a town in Galilee called Nazareth, [27]to a virgin engaged to a man whose name was Joseph, of the house of David. The virgin's name was Mary. [28]And he came to her and said, "Greetings, favored one! The Lord is with you." [29]But she was much perplexed by his words and pondered what sort of greeting this might be. [30]The angel said to her, "Do not be afraid, Mary, for you have found favor with God. [31]And now, you will conceive in your womb and bear a son, and you will name him Jesus. [32]He will be great, and will be called the Son of the Most High, and the Lord God will give to him the throne of his ancestor David. [33]He will reign over the house of Jacob forever, and of his kingdom there will be no end." [34]Mary said to the angel, "How can this be, since I am a virgin?" [35]The angel said to her, "The Holy Spirit will come upon you, and the power of the Most High will overshadow you; therefore the child to be born will be holy; he will be called Son of God. [36]And now, your relative Elizabeth in her old age has also conceived a son; and this is the sixth month for her who was said to be barren. [37]For nothing will be impossible with God." [38]Then Mary said, "Here am I, the servant of the Lord; let it be with me according to your word." Then the angel departed from her.
>
> [39]In those days Mary set out and went with haste to a Judean town in the hill country, [40]where she entered the house of Zechariah and greeted Elizabeth. [41]When Elizabeth heard Mary's greeting, the child leaped in her womb. And Elizabeth was filled with the Holy Spirit [42]and exclaimed with a loud cry, "Blessed are you among women, and blessed is the fruit of your womb. [43]And why has this happened to me, that the mother of my Lord comes to me? [44]For as soon as I heard the sound of your greeting, the child in my womb leaped for joy. [45]And blessed is she who believed that there would be a fulfillment of what was spoken to her by the Lord."
>
> [46]And Mary said, "My soul magnifies the Lord, [47]and my spirit rejoices in God my Savior, [48]for he has looked with favor on the lowliness of his servant. Surely, from now on all generations will call me blessed; [49]for the Mighty One has done great things for me, and holy is

> his name. ⁵⁰His mercy is for those who fear him from generation to generation. ⁵¹He has shown strength with his arm; he has scattered the proud in the thoughts of their hearts. ⁵²He has brought down the powerful from their thrones, and lifted up the lowly; ⁵³he has filled the hungry with good things, and sent the rich away empty. ⁵⁴He has helped his servant Israel, in remembrance of his mercy, ⁵⁵according to the promise he made to our ancestors, to Abraham and to his descendants forever." ⁵⁶And Mary remained with her about three months and then returned to her home.

YOU PUSH THE STORY

Try to identify questions about the story that help you engage it at a deeper level than you may have at other times you've encountered it. What is easy to imagine? What is difficult to understand? What do you want to know about the context of the story? What do you like about it and what makes you uncomfortable? Here are some more questions to bring you further into the story:

PUSH POSSIBILITIES FOR LUKE 1:26–56
- What is your image of Gabriel?
- What do you think of Mary's response to Gabriel's news? Does it seem realistic or simplistic?
- Why does Mary go to Elizabeth?
- What is your reaction to Mary and Elizabeth?
- Why does Mary burst out in a song of praise to God?

THE STORY PUSHES YOU

Where does this story connect with your life? How does it confirm your thoughts about call and vocation? How does it challenge you?

PUSH POSSIBILITIES FOR LUKE 1:26–56
- Mary's social status as an engaged woman changed when she responded to God's call. What social status would you be willing to give up or change to respond to a sense of call?
- There is an element of co-creation in this story. God needs Mary to bear Jesus. How do you feel about being called to be a co-creator with God?
- Mary addresses the needs and realities of her world in the song she raises to God. What would you lift up from the world today in a modern version of the "Magnificat"?

THE STORY BEHIND THE STORY

At first, the writer of the Gospel of Luke depicts Mary as surprised and afraid in the presence of the divine messenger Gabriel. Then Gabriel explains his mission and Mary is able to ask questions. In the end, Mary accepts the outrageous call of God that Gabriel brings, trusting that what the messenger says is true: Nothing is impossible with God. And, so, Mary joins the rich biblical history of God bringing special blessings to the people through chosen women, like Sarah in Genesis 15–21, Hannah in 1 Samuel 1–2, and Elizabeth in this story. In fact, this story echoes with their stories. The angel Gabriel says, "Nothing will be impossible with God," which is so similar to Sarah's, "Is anything too wonderful for the Lord?" (Genesis 18:14); and "Greetings, favored one! The Lord is with you," which is close to what the mother of Samuel, Hannah, said: "Let your servant find favor in your sight" (1 Samuel 1:18). These echoes ring assurance to Mary and to the hearers of Luke's gospel that this is part of God's plan for the people, just as those who had come before were also part of God's plan. They root this powerful new event in a powerful and trustworthy history, or unfolding, of God's salvation.

Mary's response is written in the form of a psalm or hymn. Called the "Magnificat," Mary's song of praise to God is about reversals in the *status quo*. She sings of God taking down those in power and elevating those without power. There are passages in Hebrew scripture that illuminate these themes: 1 Samuel 2:1–10, Psalm 72:12–14, and Isaiah 42:5–9. The writer of the Gospel of Luke places Mary in this stream of prophetic voices, as well as the heritage of biblical women who bear special blessings to the people. Again, the gospel is rooted in the history of God's people, bringing it forward into a new chapter with familiar and trusted themes.

We meet another woman in this passage, Elizabeth. Elizabeth is pregnant with John the Baptist. It is interesting to notice the subtle differences between their two realities and to explore the significance of their meeting. Elizabeth has been praying to conceive: She is barren and past the normal age of childbirth. Mary is a young virgin, engaged to be married. When Mary learns that Elizabeth is pregnant under such extraordinary circumstances, it serves as confirmation of what has been announced to her, equally extraordinary, though different.

> The writer of the Gospel of Luke pays particular attention to ordinary people and how God works among them to further God's purposes in the world. These two women and the men in their lives, the old priest Zechariah, married to Elizabeth, and the young carpenter Joseph, engaged to Mary, would hardly have been suspected for such enormous roles. But isn't it fitting to match the messenger to the message? Mary's song is about the lowly being lifted up and about how the usual "winners" aren't those who "win" in God's terms. It is, in fact, what happens not only through her but also to her.

PUSH OUT

- Consider reworking or paraphrasing the "Magnificat" in your own words as a way to join God's call for justice and peace in the world. How would you represent the themes of the "Magnificat" visually? Try creating a visual piece that could be used in congregational worship, as a wall hanging in a sanctuary, or as a display at a rally for peace and justice.
- Take Mary's prayer and turn it into a poem that could be presented in a service of worship or at a coffeehouse. Don't be afraid to repeat phrases that really mean something to you, and don't be afraid to use new images and contemporary language and styles.
- Make an "abilities and dreams audit" of yourself. This is an ongoing project, but if, from time to time, we consciously note these things, we might begin to see the things to which God is calling us. Take a piece of paper and draw two columns. In the first column, list your abilities. Your abilities are simply all of the things you can do. Write the big things and the small things, as many things you can think of, from riding a bike to playing a musical instrument, from reading and writing to driving a car or fixing a computer. Write down everything. Then go back and put an asterisk next to each of the abilities that people have commented on or that you truly love. For instance, many people might write down the ability to read and write, but you might put an asterisk next to reading because you love it so much or beside writing because people have commented on your poems or essays. In the second column, list the things you dream about yourself doing in the future. Be honest, no one needs to see this list but you. Beside each dream put a date as close as you can to the time when you started thinking about this. For instance, if you have dreamt of being a firefighter since you were five, put that down and a date. You might or might not decide to be a firefighter at some time in your life, but the dream of it is important and ought to be treasured. Also, remember, just because you've

only had a particular dream for a short time doesn't mean it does not have value. When you have finished your audit, hang on to it and read it often. Make some connections between things in the abilities column and things in the dreams column. You never know what new insights will come to you. Pray, too. Pray that God will show you something of God's call to you through the abilities and dreams of your life.

- Think about what you know about the way God wants the world to be. Some of this desire and plan of God's is contained in Mary's prayer (see vv. 52 and 53). Now imagine yourself in the places where you live most of your life, at home, at school, at work, with friends. Now see yourself saying what Mary said, "Here am I, the servant of the Lord; let it be with me according to your word." What might that mean to be a servant of the Lord in the places you live? What cause could you give yourself to that would be about the world becoming the way God wants it to be? Think of one thing in your home and in your work-school environment that you believe corresponds with God's desire for the world and have the courage to do it!

GROUP IDEAS

[Focus: To reinterpret "success" in God's upside-down terms, guided by Mary's song.

LIFE'S A PUSH
- Invite those in the group who are able to walk slowly around the space and to listen while the Robert Frost poem "The Road Not Taken" is read aloud.
- Discuss responses to the questions on page 115.
- Conclude with the prayer on page 116.

THE STORY
- Choose a method for your group to experience Luke 1:26–56 from the selections on page 24.
- Why not put Mary's words at the end of the reading to music or a rap or drum beat?

YOU PUSH THE STORY
- Consider the possibilities to push this story on page 118, and invite participants to come up with their own story pushes.
- As questions arise, find suggested responses in "The Story behind the Story." Also allow for group discussion.

THE STORY PUSHES YOU
- Discuss the nature of vocation. How is one called? How does one respond? Has anyone ever received such a clear message as though from a messenger of God? How does this story of Mary and her response to a call from God connect to our experience, challenge us, or invite our reflection?

PUSH OUT
- Explore the "Push Out" ideas and choose one that you might pursue as a group.

---

1. Robert Frost, "The Road Not Taken," *The Poetry of Robert Frost*, ed. Edward Connery Lathern (New York: Henry Hold & Co., 1916). Used by permission.

12. [CALLED TO THE TABLE

Jesus said, "I have come to call not the righteous but sinners to repentance."
Luke 5:32

> Jesus shares a meal with an unexpected crowd and his critics learn a valuable lesson about acceptance.

LIFE'S A PUSH

THREE STORIES

An elderly woman stands on the street corner near my office in downtown Edmonton, Canada. She's there everyday. She wears a pair of old pink sweatpants and a sloppy blue sweatshirt. She has shoulder length white hair and bushy white eyebrows. As people walk by, she smiles and says "Got a quarter?" She never asks for more than a quarter, and she always smiles in rain or sunshine. Sometimes people stop and chat with her, and at other times, they pretend not to see her, walking by without saying a word.

A teenage boy walked into an Alberta, Canada, high school with a loaded gun. He shot two boys returning from their lunch break. One of them died from the injuries. The other suffered through a long and painful recovery. Across the province, people demanded an adult trial and the maximum prison sentence for the boy who did the shooting. The parents of the boy who died, however, asked for compassion towards the young murderer.

During meetings of the Truth and Reconciliation Commission in South Africa, Archbishop Desmond Tutu heard victims share horrifying stories about their experiences at the hands of the apartheid regime. He recounts, "As well, a young one came to tell us her story of how the police detained her, and took her into a room and told her to undress, and then opened a drawer, shoved her breasts into a drawer and then slammed the drawer several times on her nipples." Tutu reflects on what he heard, "You wondered as you listened to this the depth of depravity of which we all seemed so capable, all of us. And yes, it is true, that we human beings do have an extraordinary capacity for evil."[1]

Who Is Welcome at Our Tables?

Would you share a meal with the people in these stories? Would you set a place at your table for the woman who begs on the street corner, the young man who shot and killed one of his schoolmates, or the police officers who tortured the young woman in South Africa? As you consider this question, meditate on these words from Tutu:

> None are aliens. All belong, rich and poor, white, black, red and yellow. Clever and not so clever, beautiful and not so beautiful. Rich and poor, male and female, gay and lesbian and straight. All belong, and you know something, even the awful creatures that we would like to isolate, a Hitler, a Mussolini, all of the ghastly people that inhabit our Earth, God says, you know, they too are my children and I hope that one day they would recognize that they are my children and will become what I want them to become.[2]

- How do you think Tutu would define forgiveness? acceptance?
- What patterns of exclusion are present in your life? Who are the people you have trouble accepting or forgiving?

PRAYER

Gracious God, who welcomes each and every one of us to your table of blessing, help us to be as gracious. There are those we would exclude, those we would shut out from forgiveness and compassion. Help us to see you in them and in so seeing to overcome fear, hatred, prejudice— whatever keeps us from loving as you love. Amen.

THE STORY

Jesus was often discredited for associating with sinners and "unclean" people. Read the following story from Luke 5:27–32 and reflect on how he responded to people who had a problem with his associations. You may also wish to select one of the ways to experience the story found on page 24.

> [27] After this he went out and saw a tax collector name Levi, sitting at the tax booth; and he said to him, "Follow me." [28] And he got up, left everything, and followed him. [29] Then Levi gave a great banquet for him in his house; and there was a large crowd of tax collectors and others sitting at the table with them. [30] The Pharisees and their scribes were complaining to his disciples, saying, "Why do you eat and drink with tax collectors and sinners?" [31] Jesus answered, "Those who are well have no need of a physician, but those who are sick; [32] I have come to call not the righteous but sinners to repentance."

YOU PUSH THE STORY

Take some time to reflect on this story. What interests you about the relationship between Jesus and the other characters? What parts of the story make you uncomfortable? Consider the following questions and others that emerge for you.

PUSH POSSIBILITIES FOR LUKE 5:27–32

- Why does Levi throw a huge banquet for Jesus?
- Why do the Pharisees and scribes complain about the guest list?
- Whom is Jesus calling to repentance in this story? Why does he think they need to repent?
- What role did tax collectors play in ancient Palestine? How was the role abused?
- Why did Jesus associate with tax collectors?
- What did physicians in ancient times do for people who needed healing?
- What does the word "righteous" mean? Who are the righteous ones in the story?

THE STORY PUSHES YOU

Think about what this story has to say about you and your values. How does it challenge your priorities and the way you relate to other people? Consider how the story empowers, offers hope, and creates new insights.

PUSH POSSIBILITIES FOR LUKE 5:27–32

- Who do you identify with in this story—Levi, the tax collectors, the Pharisees, the scribes, the disciples, or Jesus?
- Why would Jesus call Levi to follow him? When have you felt called by God?

- What might Levi have given up in order to follow Jesus? What might people have to give up in order to follow Jesus today?
- What is repentance and what might it involve for people today?
- What illness did Jesus come to heal? What illnesses need to be healed in our society?
- Who are the righteous ones in our society? Who are the sinners?

THE STORY BEHIND THE STORY

Tax collectors are rarely popular in any culture at any time. However, the tax collectors of ancient Palestine may have been especially despised. Find out why in what follows.

The Romans financed their empire with taxes levied against the peoples they conquered. Roman officials in Palestine farmed out the task of collecting the taxes to local entrepreneurs known as "publicans." Levi may have been one of those co-opted publicans. He probably collected tolls from his own people who were transporting property by land or sea. Whatever amount of money he collected, on top of the basic tax, was his to keep. Levi might have been among those publicans who kept a lot!

Jesus invites Levi to follow him. He does so, leaving everything behind him. The story tells us that Levi gave a "great feast" for a "host of friends." This indicates that he was a wealthy man. Jesus is specifically honored at this feast. Tax collectors and others attended the meal. The "others" were unlikely to have been Pharisees and scribes because they probably would not have attended a meal hosted by someone considered a traitor to their own people. Publicans were wealthy outcasts who would have been denied access to the temple.

In many cultures, sharing a meal with someone meant that you accepted them. The Pharisees in this story rebuked the disciples of Jesus because they shared table fellowship with sinners. In speaking to the disciples rather than to Jesus, the religious leaders were aiming their criticism at the faith community forming around Jesus.

Jesus says that he is calling all sinners to "repentance." In the Bible, this word is defined in many ways. It includes regret and changing one's mind or actively turning away from a particular behavior or attitude. In Christian scripture, true repentance leads to forgiveness for sins.

"Those who are well have no need of a physician, but those who are sick," says Jesus in Luke 5:31b. In this statement, Jesus indirectly compares himself to the professional healers that were common in ancient Israel. These healers were known to apply many practical remedies to

> injuries and illnesses. These treatments included bandages, salves, and poultices. Prayer was also included in these remedies.
>
> Christian scripture portrays Jesus as healing many illnesses through a laying on of hands and intercessory prayer. Luke 5:27–32 suggests that in this particular case, many sins needed healing, including greed, fraud (in the matter of taxes), self-righteousness, and exclusion.

PUSH OUT

Find ways to explore expressions of Jesus' healing ministry in our world today. Some possibilities might include the following:

- Learn more about repentance as a lived reality in our society and look for ways to support these efforts. For instance, does your church participate in victim and offender reconciliation programs? How is repentance expressed both verbally and in practical terms in these situations? How is the larger church involved in supporting true change in the behavior of offenders?
- Is your denomination involved in healing the wounds caused by colonization and the oppression of native peoples? Gather information and facilitate an educational event to call attention to these efforts.
- Jesus was often accused of standing with the outcasts in society. Are there ways that your group might offer assistance to those who are friendless and lonely? Who are they in your community, and who else is helping them that your group might support or join?
- If your group is particularly interested in the issue of healing from sin, you may want to close this session with the following ritual. Give people slips of paper and pencils. Invite them to write some of the sins for which they want God's forgiveness on one side of their slips of paper. On the other side, ask them to name the ways in which they will turn away from that behavior or attitude in the future and any plans they have to bring about healing. Burn the slips of paper in a metal bowl. As the paper turns to ash, say a healing prayer such as the following:

> ### PRAYER
> God, we ask your healing touch upon each of us. Forgive us when we turn away from your love, and help us turn from actions that do not share your love with others. Help us to open our hearts to those cast out by the world around us. Help us be your welcoming people. Amen.

GROUP IDEAS

Focus: To reflect on how we can bring about acceptance, repentance, and healing in society and ourselves.

LIFE'S A PUSH
- Invite three different people to read aloud the stories provided. Ask for the group's reactions to the stories. Then discuss the question, "Would you share a meal with the people in these stories?" Continue the conversation by having one person read aloud the quote from Desmond Tutu. First, reflect on the quote silently, then discuss the additional questions provided.

THE STORY
- Choose a method for your group to use for reading the Luke passage from the selections on page 24.
- Alternatively, have volunteers read aloud the parts of the narrator, Jesus, and the Pharisees and scribes. Afterwards, discuss how it felt to assume those parts.

YOU PUSH THE STORY
- What disturbs you about Luke 5:27–32? Brainstorm any questions that you have about the passage. Also consider the push possibilities for Luke 5:27–32.
- Review "The Story behind the Story" as a group to see if it responds to any concerns and questions that have been raised.

THE STORY PUSHES YOU
- Discuss the ways people in the group responded to the characters in the story. How did the characters connect to members' experiences? Discuss the other questions provided. Take note of which questions created the most heated debate. Plan to come back to them in a future discussion.

PUSH OUT
- Have the group choose one of the "Push Out" ideas. Make concrete plans together to act on it.
- Close with a ritual or the prayer provided.

---

1. Desmond Tutu, "What Was Said: 'We Have an Extraordinary Capacity for God,'" *Edmonton Journal*, 14 June 2000. A15.
2. Ibid.

13. [WHO IS MY NEIGHBOR?

You shall love the Lord your God with all your heart, and with all your soul, with all your strength, and with all your mind; and your neighbor as yourself.

Luke 10:27

When a lawyer cross-examines Jesus about what's really important, he gets an answer he may not have bargained for. If we ever find ourselves asking what matters most, what do we do with the answers? How do we live the love that is at the heart of our faith?

LIFE'S A PUSH

KEEPING THE FAITH

Gien stands by the piano, holding her plump baby girl on one hip with one hand, running the fingers of the other hand lightly along the silent white keys. Before the war, she and Frits gathered with friends around the gleaming walnut piano and sang country songs celebrating the sea of grain in the farmers' fields. But since the Nazis marched into Amsterdam, yellow stars hastily sewn onto jackets and dresses have replaced the yellow grain. She no longer has a taste for sweet words and folk music.

Gien's own star is hidden by false identity papers, the gift of her Gentile husband's sister. Today the small living room with its white lace curtains feels claustrophobic. She steps out onto the balcony that they share with their landlord. His balcony door is open, as always, and she sees him leaning against the railing. A cool breeze ruffles her long brown hair. He looks over at her and gravely tips his beaten straw hat. She smiles and, for a moment, feels free.

Mieke Wharton is Gien Meyer's daughter. Her mother's maiden name was Cohen, and she was a Jew passing as a Gentile during the Nazi occupation. "The Germans announced that all Jews in Holland had to wear a yellow star," says Mieke. "But my mother chose not to wear it." Gien knew that the price of disclosure was high—early in the war, her parents had obeyed orders, worn the yellow star, and were murdered in the death camps. "My aunt gave my mother her identification papers," says Mieke. "This worked well because my aunt was unmarried and, of course, had the same last name as my father."

The Meyer's developed an escape route in case Gien's secret was discovered. "Our landlord was the only person outside of our family who knew that my mother was Jewish," says Mieke. "We lived in an apartment next door to his and shared an adjoining balcony with him. He always kept the door on his side of the balcony unlocked. If the soldiers came to get her, she was to slip into his house, put on a disguise he had prepared for her, and go out through his front door."

Fortunately, Gien Meyer never had to use this escape route. Her landlord always kept her secret, and none of her other neighbors ever learned why Gien Meyer always seemed so reserved and melancholy. When asked why her parents' non-Jewish landlord supported them, Mieke is silent for a moment. "I think he understood what they faced. After the war, I learned that he was gay. . . . "[1]

- Gien Meyer's landlord kept her secret and provided her with an escape route. When you've been in a difficult situation, who has been a neighbor to you?

PRAYER

God, who is with us in our deepest fears and most painful moments, be with us today in our reflections on faith and life. May we find the strength to live out our faith, even when we ourselves are living life on the margins. Amen

Consider another ancient story about a neighbor who reaches out, despite the risk to himself.

THE STORY

Read the story from Luke 10:25–37. This story lends itself to a dramatic reading ("performing" the dialogue in different voices with a narrator)—or select another way to experience it from the suggestions found on page 24.

> [25]Just then a lawyer stood up to test Jesus. "Teacher," he said "what must I do to inherit eternal life?" [26]He said to him, "What is written in the law? What do you read there?" [27]He answered, "You shall love the Lord your God with all your heart, and with all your soul, and with all your mind; and your neighbor as yourself." [28]And he said to him, "You have given the right answer; do this, and you will live."

Who Is My Neighbor?

> ²⁹But wanting to justify himself, he asked Jesus, " And who is my neighbor?" ³⁰Jesus replied, "A man was going down form Jerusalem to Jericho, and fell into the hands of robbers, who stripped him, beat him, and went away, leaving him half dead. ³¹Now by chance a priest was going down that road; and when he saw him, he passed by on the other side. ³²So likewise a Levite, when he came to the place and saw him, passed by on the other side. ³³But a Samaritan while traveling came near him; and when he saw him, he was moved with pity. ³⁴He went to him and bandaged his wounds, having poured oil and wine on them. Then he put him on his own animal, brought him to an inn, and took care of him. ³⁵The next day he took out two denarii, gave them to the innkeeper, and said, 'Take care of him; and when I come back, I will repay you whatever more you spend.' ³⁶Which of these three, do you think, was a neighbor to the man who fell into the hands of the robbers?" ³⁷He said, "The one who showed him mercy." Jesus said to him, "Go and do likewise."

YOU PUSH THE STORY

Think about the story for a moment. With which characters do you identify? What questions does the story raise for you? Explore ways that the story compels you, creates tension or confusion, or gives you an "aha" or fresh insight.

PUSH POSSIBILITIES FOR LUKE 10:25–37

- Who were the Samaritans? What difference does it make for the man of the story to be a Samaritan?
- Why didn't the religious leaders stop and help the injured man?
- What does this story suggest about religious leaders of the past and present? about the practices of faith past and present?
- What does it mean to have eternal life?
- What do you imagine the lawyer doing if he were to "go and do likewise"?

THE STORY PUSHES YOU

Reflect on what this story may have to say about our relationships and our actions towards other people. Think about what it means to live out your faith towards those you may not even know.

PUSH POSSIBILITIES FOR LUKE 10:25-37

- What does the statement "Love the Lord your God with all your heart, and with all your soul, with all your strength and with all your mind; and your neighbor as yourself," mean to you?
- Who are the Samaritans in our society? Who are the victims?
- What modern situations call for healing?
- When have you felt like the victim left lying at the side of the road? What were you going through? Who helped you?
- What might prevent you from stopping to help someone if they were lying on the side of the road? When have you helped someone who was either literally or figuratively robbed? Why did you help?

THE STORY BEHIND THE STORY

After Assyrian invaders swept the kingdom of Israel under their chariot wheels in the eighth century B.C.E., the new rulers initiated a policy of ethnic cleansing. Thirty thousand of the wealthiest and most influential leaders among the people of Israel were deported to the northern Euphrates. They were replaced by unwilling immigrants from Babylon, Cuthah, Hamath, Avya, and Sepharvaim—mystical sounding places in what is now Syria and Iraq. Forcibly resettled by the Assyrians, these groups adjusted to new lives in the shadow of Mount Gerazim.

During the time of Christ, a small community of Samaritans was living in that region. Their name comes from the city of Samaria, Israel's capital triumphantly conquered by the Assyrians in 721 B.C.E., following a bloody three-year siege. The Samaritans believed themselves to be descended from the northern Israelite tribes of Ephraim and Manasseh. The Pentateuch (the first five books of the Hebrew Bible) was their holy book, and they considered themselves to be decedents of Jacob. But unlike their sisters and brothers in the south, they regarded Mount Gerazim—not Jerusalem—as the place set aside for making sacrifices to God.

Despite shared beliefs and signs of a shared heritage, the Jews of Jesus' time regarded the Samaritans as foreigners—remnants of the unwilling migrants settled in the north by the Assyrians. Such foreigners (including Samaritans) were considered ritually unclean and excluded from participation in the Jerusalem temple. For their part, the Samaritans considered the Jews to be heretics who long ago established a rival sanctuary away from God's holy mountain.

A Samaritan is at the heart of the story told by Jesus in Luke 10:25–37. His actions toward a robbery victim on a lonely stretch of road between Jericho and Jerusalem are contrasted with those of a priest and a Levite. Levites were temple assistants who maintained order in the Jerusalem temple, acted as doorkeepers, and killed sacrificial animals. Priests were on an even higher rung on the Jewish liturgical ladder—only they were allowed to approach the holy altar and perform the rituals surrounding animal sacrifices.

One of the most important tasks of the priest was to maintain the purity of the temple. In Jesus' story, a ritually "unclean" Samaritan offers assistance to an injured man while a priest walks past "on the other side." The lawyer listening to the story learns that it is the Samaritan who faithfully lives out the love commandment. This startling conclusion—that the most impure person is our neighbor who demands a response—could have overturned the deeply held religious concerns and assumptions of Jesus' listeners. This was precisely what the story was intended to do. The experience of the Samaritan, so often portrayed in Jesus' stories, symbolized what it meant to be faithful in challenging terms.

PUSH OUT

Chose one of the following ideas to help you further explore the story of the Good Samaritan and to reflect on the kind of neighbor each of us is called by our faith to be.

- Retell the story as a play set in modern times. Who is the contemporary Samaritan? Who are the other characters, recast in modern terms? What's the setting? What situation will the robbery victim face? Why will people fail to help their neighbor? Use the drama in worship with your faith community or at the beginning of your study session.
- Establish a "Samaritan Bible Study." Look through the Bible for other Samaritan stories and explore them with a study group. How are the Samaritans portrayed? How did their role change over time? Why did Jesus use them as examples in his stories? What message was he trying to convey?
- In a study group or book club, explore the parallels between a contemporary story and the biblical story of the Good Samaritan. (You may want to look at books by Alice Walker, Margaret Laurence, James Baldwin, Maya Angelou, Walker Percy, or Margaret Atwood.)

- Host a movie night for a group. Watch the film *Life is Beautiful* or *The Red Violin*. Talk about the life stories revealed in the movie you choose. Who are the heroes in the film? What sacrifices do they make on behalf of others? Which characters seem unsure of themselves in responding to difficult situations? Which characters turn away from caring for their fellow human beings? Who chooses to harm others, and what do they gain doing do?
- The Samaritan brought the robbery victim to a local inn and paid the owner to take care of him. Homelessness is a major problem in North America and around the world. In cities like New York and Toronto, people make their homes in cardboard boxes just outside the entrances to expensive restaurants. Teenagers living on the street wash car windows to earn enough money to buy a decent meal. Consider lending support to the efforts of groups who are trying to help people find refuge from life on the streets. Perhaps start with this internationally active group:

Habitat for Humanity (U.S.A.)
121 Habitat St
Americus GA 31709-3498
800.422.4828
www.habitat.org

Habitat for Humanity (Canada)
40 Albert St
Waterloo, Ontario
Canada N2L 3S2
800.667.5137

Who Is My Neighbor?   135

GROUP IDEAS

Focus: To find new ways to "go and do likewise" in terms of loving our neighbors.

LIFE'S A PUSH
- Gather the group to sit in a circle. Place an object that you associate with being a "Good Samaritan" on a table or on the floor in the center of the circle. Consider one of these or something similar: a ribbon or button representing a local charity or cause, a box of Girl Scout cookies, an offering basket from a worship community; congregational or denominational outreach or mission event announcements. As you're arranging the centerpiece, invite group members to describe other things that remind them of "Good Samaritans."
- Ask people to say the first thing that comes into their minds when they hear the word "neighbor." Have someone read the story of Regina Meyer to the group. Ask the group to discuss the landlord's actions—why did he do what he did?
- Say the prayer on page 130 or one of yours.

THE STORY
- Invite someone in your group to tell the story of the Good Samaritan from memory. Then have the group read "The Story" and talk about what points in the retelling may have been missing and what was not forgotten. Alternatively, encourage people to name what is the most memorable part of the story for them, and what feelings the story evokes. Then have someone read "The Story" to the group.
- Choose a method for your group to read and experience Luke 10:25–37 from the suggestions on page 24.

YOU PUSH THE STORY
- Select some of the push possibilities for the group to use in reflecting on the story in Luke 10:25–37.
- Invite the group to identify their doubts, concerns, and questions about the story. Refer to background material in "The Story behind the Story" for information that can help the group work with the push possibilities and what they bring to the story themselves.

THE STORY PUSHES YOU
- Discuss some of the push possibilities offered on page 131.
- Invite group members to talk about other ways that the story challenges them to reflect on their lives.

PUSH OUT
- Choose one or more of the "Push Out" ideas and make whatever preparations you need to in order to involve the group.
- Close the gathering by inviting participants to jot down the names of people they know who are struggling with difficult challenges and people who are trying to heal the wounded in your community. Include these names in the closing prayer, either the one offered below or of your own creation.

> **PRAYER**
> Thank you God, for the people who heal the wounded in our community. We remember *(name those who care for others in your community)*. We also pray for those who have been hurt and feel alone, away from human care. Bless *(name those who are experiencing pain, loss, or abandonment)*. Strengthen us to love our neighbors as we love ourselves and to experience your guiding love. Amen.

---

1. Debbie Culbertson, "Keeping the Faith in Alberta," *Alberta Views Magazine* 4, no. 6 (Nov/Dec. 2002), 44–48.

14. [FAITH WORKS

For just as the body without the spirit is dead, so faith without works is also dead.

>> James 2:26

> Truth matters when it is risked in action. The letter from James challenges us to risk our trust in God with action.

LIFE'S A PUSH

TRYING SOMETHING

I had just turned 18. I wondered a lot about what I was supposed to do with my life. When I thought about it, I felt paralyzed. Too many ideas. Too many voices. It was the end of summer and I was on a road trip to a different city. My traveling companions and I had stopped at a tourist information booth. I spotted a man sprawled Gumby-doll-like in the middle of three lanes of traffic. He was calling out, but we couldn't understand what he was saying. One of the people I was with said, "He's drunk. Let's call the police."

Somebody else said, "What are we supposed to do with him?"

During a lull in the traffic, I ran out into the street to where he was lying. His pant legs were twisted inside the joints of his artificial legs. He was drunk and he said to me, "Just go and leave me here. Don't waste your time on me." While I struggled to help him up, two other men who knew him pulled up in a van, perpendicular to the flow of traffic. The men helped me get him into the van, and they took him safely away. I was glad I stepped out into that street and took some action. Somehow, it made the big questions in life not so paralyzing.

LEARN HOW TO USE MY HANDS

The Indigo Girls sing a song, "Hammer and a Nail," about putting ideas into action:

Gotta get out of bed get a hammer and a nail
Learn how to use my hands, not just my head
I think myself into jail
Now I know a refuge never grows
From a chin in a hand in a thoughtful pose
Gotta tend the earth if you want a rose.

I had a lot of good intentions
Sit around for fifty years and then collect a pension,
Start seeing the road to hell and just where it starts.
But my life is more than a vision
The sweetest part is acting after making a decision
I started seeing the whole as a sum of its parts.

My life is a part of the global life
I'd found myself becoming more immobile
when I'd think a little girl in the world can't do anything
A distant nation my community
A street person my responsibility
If I have a care in the world I have a gift to bring.[1]

A Christmas Present

It was Christmas day. Julie sat in church with her parents and her two brothers. In her hands, she held the two most precious presents that she had received under the tree that morning. It was the tradition in her church for the pastor to ask the children of the congregation to show some of their gifts. In one hand, Julie held a small diary that her aunt had given her to write her thoughts in. It had a brass clasp and a tiny padlock with a key. In the other hand, she held five, brand-new ten-dollar notes, a gift from her grandparents who lived too far away to be with their grandchildren on Christmas day. Julie listened to the service, the singing of hymns of praise, and the thanks to God, and she listened to the story told of the children in Rwanda who not only would not have enough money for presents this Christmas but would not even have enough for basic food. In one moment, Julie realized that she held in her hand a way of helping those children and of also expressing her joy and thankfulness for Christmas and the coming of Jesus. With little more than a moment's thought about the joy she might be able to bring, Julie ran forward from her place in the congregation and placed her crisp new notes in the collection bowl.

THE TAIZE COMMUNITY: AN ACT OF FAITH

It was 1940. The Second World War was raging all across Europe; people everywhere were on the move trying to escape the fighting. In France, those who could were leaving, trying to find safety. Roger, a young man in his twenties, decided to go the other way, toward the fighting, into France from his native and safe Switzerland. Roger was motivated by a deep felt desire for reconciliation fueled by stories of his grandmother who sheltered refugees during the dark days of the previous war.

Roger was looking for a house in which to put into practice, in a small way, his hopes and desires about community and reconciliation. Welcomed to the tiny village of Taize by an old woman, he bought a small house and began providing shelter for political refugees. At the conclusion of the war, Brother Roger gathered a small number of young men who, like himself, wanted to live a simple communal life. So began what is now internationally known as a community of reconciliation for all. What began in a small house in a tiny village in the midst of a terrible war has grown into a place of pilgrimage for thousands and thousands of people, particularly young people, all holding a deep desire that their communities and nations be reconciled and that love be at the heart of all human interaction.

- Can you think of an experience when things became clearer to you by just doing something?
- How do you relate to the "analysis paralysis" of stuck decision-making in the opening story or in the song "Hammer and a Nail"?
- Do religious beliefs require decisions and actions, or are they merely to be accepted "as is" on the basis of some authority, be it tradition, scripture, parents, or community?

PRAYER

Some are of the opinion
That their success to love is great
So all the world blooms for them
And turns green.
But then we learn the truth
And see that it is not so:
For it is only our works of faithfulness
That prove our progress in love.[2]

A letter of the early church challenges the idea that it is enough to simply accept and say that you believe certain things. The writer of this story describes a faith that has the power to give life because it is chosen and acted on.

THE STORY

Read the story from James 2:14–6. What can you determine about the two sides of the debate at the heart of this passage? Consider writing summary statements for the opposing arguments as though you were being called on to defend each one. Or, choose one or two ways to experience the passage more fully from the ideas on page 24.

> [14]What good is it, my brothers and sisters, if you say you have faith but do not have works? Can faith save you? [15]If a brother or sister is naked and lacks daily food, [16]and one of you says to them, "Go in peace; keep warm and eat your fill," and yet you do not supply their bodily needs, what is the good of that? [17]So faith by itself, if it has no works, is dead. [18]But someone will say, "You have faith and I have works." Show me your faith apart from your works, and I by my works will show you my faith. [19]You believe that God is one; you do well. Even the demons believe—and shudder. [20]Do you want to be shown, you senseless person, that faith apart from works is barren? [21]Was not our ancestor Abraham justified by works when he offered his son Isaac on the altar? [22]You see that faith was active along with his works, and faith was brought to completion by the works. [23]Thus the scripture was fulfilled that says, "Abraham believed God, and it was reckoned to him as righteousness," and he was called the friend of God. [24]You see that a person is justified by works and not by faith alone. [25]Likewise, was not Rahab the prostitute also justified by works when she welcomed the messengers and sent them out by another road? [26]For just as the body without the spirit is dead, so faith without works is also dead.

YOU PUSH THE STORY

Raise questions about the passage from James, its content and context. Push any possible inconsistencies or contradictions you see. Press the language of James with your doubts and your hopes. Begin with the suggestions below. There is discussion around these suggestions included in "The Story behind the Story" on pages 141–42.

Push Possibilities for James 2:14–26
- Romans 3:28 reads, "For we hold that a person is justified by faith apart from works prescribed by the law." Is James making the opposite case?
- What does "faith" mean in James?
- Who is Rahab?
- What does Abraham have to do with this story?
- Who is the writer arguing with and calling a "senseless person"?
- What's the business about shuddering demons?

The Story Pushes You
Consider how the story may push your understanding of faith and your living of it.

Push Possibilities for James 2:14–26
- Does the letter of James suggest that faith may have more to do with actions on behalf of the poor rather than moral piety?
- According to James, is faith more than an emotional feeling of being close to God, having a positive outlook, or simple assent to certain doctrines? What do you believe?
- How does this story invite you to read the Bible in a way that holds what seem to be contradictions and two sides of a question in tension with one another?
- What kinds of actions does the story challenge you to take?
- What does the story mean for those seeking a faith community? What does it say about how to "be church"?
- How does the story offer challenge, hope, empowerment?

> ### THE STORY BEHIND THE STORY
> The letter of James was written as a general message to all Christians (rather than to any one particular community) about how to live out faith. The writer is particularly interested in defining faith according to some very specific actions, including visiting the orphan and the widow in affliction (1:27), respecting the poor (2:6), controlling the tongue (1:26), feeding the hungry, and having patience (5:7).
>
> In the Protestant tradition, in particular, a lot has been said about "salvation by grace through faith," an argument supported by passages written by the apostle Paul to churches in Rome, Galatia, and Corinth. Paul wrote often about his belief that the works of the law were not the way to salvation. He addressed what he considered to be the starting point of faith—the way in which we are brought into right relationship

with God through the gift of grace. James might be seen as addressing the continued life of the believer, rather than this starting point. Read together this way, the arguments of Paul and James are not a contrast of faith and works.

The letter of James is addressing a contrast, however—the contrast between genuine faith and fake faith. The writer is concerned with "cheap grace," or talking a good talk without walking the walk of faith-empowered living. Works are what make faith come alive, though they alone do not give us relationship with God. There is a symbiotic relationship between the gift of grace and the acts of faith that give fullness to our relationship with God and to our faithful living in the world. Works are the fruit of faith. In chapter 2, verse 20, the word "barren" may also be translated "fruitless." It doesn't produce anything.

The writer of the letter of James uses a rhetorical device in which a "straw man" is set up for the sake of argument. There may be no actual person or group with whom the author is arguing, but this is a way of making a point. In arguing, the writer creates a number of specific examples. We can say all the right things, such as "God is one" and we can fear God. But even the demons that Jesus encounters in the gospel can speak the truth of faith and "shudder," such as the demon that says, "What have you to do with us, Jesus of Nazareth . . . I know who you are, the Holy One of God" (Mark 1:24), and is afraid. But the demon doesn't act in ways consistent with faith.

Abraham is used as an example of one willing to act out of faith, ready to sacrifice his only son Isaac before God provides for a way for Isaac to be spared. The writer quotes Genesis about "reckoned to him as righteousness" from the story of Abraham trusting that God would offer Sarah and him a son, Isaac, even before they had any proof that such a promise could possibly be fulfilled. The letter also includes the example of Rahab, a character from the book of Joshua, who takes in the Israelite spies and hides them in her house while the men of Jericho search for them. It's especially notable that Rahab's faith in action is held up because, as a prostitute, she was considered an outsider to the religious circles.

PUSH OUT

Faith works allow faith to work. The work of faith gives the power to faith. Consider how to experience this truth in one or more of the suggested "Push Out" ideas.

- The movie *Shadowlands* is about a famous Christian thinker, C. S. Lewis, who talks a lot about God's love as that "which chisels us into shape." Lewis lives an isolated life of ideas and words until he falls in love with a woman who shows him what the joy and the struggle of love is truly about. View *Shadowlands* (HBO Canada, 1993; director, Richard Attenbrough) and discuss how the character of C. S. Lewis is transformed by living out the hard realities of love.
- If faith goes together with works, then prayer goes together with action. Contemplation and action can be thought of as two sides of the same coin. Share with others things you have done vocationally, as a volunteer, or spontaneously that helped you understand things differently. How did some of these experiences change you spiritually or change how you communicate with or know God's presence? What spiritual disciplines might ground you even more in the things that you do in your work, with your family, or as a community member?
- The story of James speaks of "supplying the bodily needs" of those who are naked and lack daily food. Make a list of all the ways you have encountered people in the last week or two who, in some way, are naked and lack daily food. Then create another list of the things you are good at. Compare the two and see where there might be some corresponding calls to action. How might your skills and talents meet these needs? Choose something to do as an act of faith, together with others or on your own. After one experience, discern whether there is some ongoing commitment you could make to this kind of "faith in action" or something similar.
- Can you think of contemporary music that speaks to ideas put into action? Spend time listening to these songs for inspiration.
- Our work lives can have profound connections to our spiritual lives. A living wage, health care, safety and freedom from health hazards on the job, opportunities for free time and Sabbath, and dignity in work are all basic human rights as articulated in the "Universal Declaration of Human Rights." Many communities have coalitions among labor unions and faith communities that work together to protect these rights and reflect on the relationships between faith and work. Find out if there is such a coalition in your area and learn about what they do. How can you get involved? Check out the Web site of the National Interfaith Committee for Worker Justice at <www.nicwj.org> or write, 1020 West Bryn Mawr Avenue, 4th Floor, Chicago, Illinois, 60660.

GROUP IDEAS

Focus: To experience the power of faith by risking its expression in action.

LIFE'S A PUSH
- Place in the center of your gathering space pictures of persons engaged in acts of compassion and caring. Ask group members to reflect on the images.
- Read both the story "Trying Something" and the lyrics to "Hammer and a Nail."
- Discuss the questions included in "Life's a Push" on page 139.
- Offer the prayer from page 139 or a prayer of yours.

THE STORY
- Read together the story from James.
- Select a method from the suggestions on page 24 for experiencing the story. Working with words or sorting through the debate it raises are two good choices for this passage.

YOU PUSH THE STORY
- Invite participants to raise questions about the story.
- Include some of the push possibilities listed on page 141 in the discussion.
- Divide into groups to explore responses to some of the questions raised by the material in "The Story behind the Story."
- Have groups report back to the whole group.

THE STORY PUSHES YOU
- Suggest taking five minutes of silence to meditate on ways the story offers challenge, hope, and renewal.
- Come back together as a group and share discoveries.

PUSH OUT
- Share the list of ideas for a "Push Out" with the group and together decide on one or more experiences.
- As a closing, offer the prayer below from W. E. B. DuBois or invite a member of the group to reflect on the hope encountered in pushing this story from James.

> **PRAYER**
>
> Give us grace, O God, to dare to do the deed that we well know cries out to be done. Let us not hesitate because of ease, or the words of men's and women's mouths, or our own lives. Mighty causes are calling us. Amen.[3]

---

1. Indigo Girls, *Nomads Indians Saints* (CBS Records, Epic, 1990). Used by permission.
2. Hadewijch of Brabant (1204–1244), *Prayers for the Common Good*, ed. A. Jean Lesher (Cleveland: The Pilgrim Press, 1998), 150.
3. W. E. B. DuBois, in William D. Lindsey, *Singing in a Strange Land: Praying and Acting with the Poor* (Kansas City, Mo.: Sheed and Ward, 1991), 21.

CONTRIBUTORS

JANA NORMAN, editor for *Push It!* volume 3, is the minister for curriculum development, Local Church Ministries, a Covenanted Ministry of the United Church of Christ in Cleveland, Ohio.

SIDNEY D. FOWLER wrote the introduction, "What's the Push All About?" He is the minister for worship, liturgy, and spiritual formation, Local Church Ministries, a Covenanted Ministry of the United Church of Christ in Cleveland, Ohio.

TOM CHU, program director for the Ministries with Young People Cluster at the Episcopal Church Center in New York, is the writer for sessions 1, 5, and 11.

CRAIG SCHAUB, wrote sessions 2, 3, 4, 7, 8, 9, and 14. He also wrote the article, "Ideas for Deepening the Connection to the Bible." Craig is pastor of Plymouth Congregational United Church of Christ in Syracuse, New York.

DEBBIE CULBERTSON is the writer of sessions 6, 10, 12, 13, and "How to Use *Push It!*" She is a writer, editor, and publisher living in Spruce Grove, Alberta, Canada, and a member of the United Church of Canada.